THE BIG GAME

The Big Game

Things Men
SHOULD
Talk About But Rarely Do

PERRY UNDERWOOD

THE BIG GAME

ISBN-13:978-1534957121

ISBN-10:153495712X

TABLE OF CONTENTS

ACKNOWLEDGMENTS

My thanks go to Rob Fischer, friend and editor of this book. Thanks
to Kim Gardell for layout and design.
Thanks to friends and brother:
Rob Fischer, Robert Harper, Pat McHugh, Mike O'Connor
and Doug Underwood
for reviewing this book before publication.
Your work, comments and feedback were invaluable.

A special thanks to my wife, Susan
for walking beside me for thirty-eight years
and for her role in helping write a
better story for my life.
She plays a significant role in several of these stories
and my hope is that she never reads any of them.

This book is dedicated to my dad.

INTRODUCTION

MY FAVORITE MOVIES TEND TO be those that are based on true stories of how ordinary men have changed the world. When I look at our movie collection I see movies like *"42"* the story of Jackie Robinson becoming the first black to play in MLB; *"Glory Road"* the story of Texas Western University Coach Don Haskins' battle to feature black basketball players in the NCAA; *"Remember the Titans"* the story of Coach Bill Yoast's triumphant integration of black football players into a whites only High School football league.

And then there are other great movies such as *"Sergeant York"* the WWI hero of the Battle of Argonne; and *"Amazing Grace"* the story of William Wilberforce and his life-long efforts to bring the slave trade and eventually slavery itself to an end throughout the British Empire. And of course no list would be complete without including *"Schindler's List."*

How is it that ordinary men can live in such a way that movies are made about their lives, sometimes long after they are dead?

I wonder if any of the men named above had any inkling that they were making history at the time they were in the midst of their battle? They were just men who were doing what they knew to be right. They were men driven by justice and history has rewarded their courage.

Patrick Morley wrote, "A man's most innate need is his need to be significant – to find purpose and meaning."

But as men, how do we go about finding our purpose? How do we find a life full of meaning? How are we to be relevant in a world where we have little if any control? What if it really is true that every man has the drive to be a man of significance? But what if it is also true that every man has within his DNA the ability to change the world?

My inspiration for writing *The Big Game* came from the book *A Million Miles in a Thousand Years* by Donald Miller, a book referred to me by my friend Neil Ziegler. Miller's book is the story of how his earlier book, *Blue Like Jazz* had been made into a movie. What struck me most as I read *A Million Miles in a Thousand Years* was that our life is a story. No matter what may have happened in our past, with every new day we have the opportunity to write a new chapter to our story or possibly even write a whole new story.

Miller asks what our story would look like if it were made into a movie. Would our story make a hit movie or even an interesting one? Or would our story be one that was so dull that the screen-writers couldn't find anything worth making into a movie and just throw our story into the trash? Miller believes that even though our life story may have been boring or even dreadful, as long as we're alive, we still have opportunity to create an ending that could make our story a blockbuster. I couldn't agree with him more.

Now I'm not suggesting that in writing our story we have control of how things will turn out in the end. Each day our life story encounters new twists and challenges that we could have never anticipated. But each day we also make hundreds of decisions that will influence the next scene or the next chapter. It is how we deal with these unexpected twists and challenges that make our story interesting.

Most great movies have a main character that is triumphant over adversity or an impossible situation. Movies about sports teams are more powerful when the winning team has overcome impossible odds and began their journey as a huge underdog. In the movie *Rocky* the Italian Stallion, Rocky Balboa didn't even win in the end. But he put up such an incredible fight against his overwhelmingly favored opponent that every man who's ever seen the movie will forever remember the line by Apollo Creed, "Ain't gonna be no rematch."

I've chosen *The Big Game* as the title of this book; it is a play on words. Men talk about so many things and when we hear *The Big Game* it could be in reference to a sporting event, hunting, work, or just life in general. But the reality is that most men are just playing with each other. In other words, we men tend to talk about everything under the sun except the things that we really need to talk about and that really matter the most.

As men we tend to want to be independent and tough. We might get together with other guys and watch a football game, go hunting, grab a beer after work, kick back at a BBQ or maybe even do a Bible Study. But what do we really know about these other guys…and just as important, what do they really know about us? How are the men who are closest to us helping us write a better story for our lives and how are we helping them write a better story for theirs?

My Dad was a minister so I grew up in church and have been attending church my entire life. I have been involved with Men's Ministries and Men's Groups throughout the years. The typical Men's Ministry involves a bunch of guys getting together for breakfast one Saturday each month to hang out, enjoy some small talk about "the game" or whatever, hear a mini-sermon from a guest speaker and then head out to our normal Saturday routine. Then there are Men's Groups. Men's Groups usually involve meeting at some ungodly early morning hour one day each week and reading a chapter from the Bible or some other inspirational book and then sharing our thoughts and opinions for the remainder of our allotted time. Please don't get me wrong, I'm not being critical. As a matter of fact often times it was me who was leading such a Ministry or Group. But I've learned that there is so much more and I can no longer settle for less.

When it comes to hunting, going to a game, or grabbing a beer do we really know these guys we're hanging out and shooting the breeze with? The same question applies to Men's Ministries or Men's Groups. Some of these Men's Ministry Saturday morning breakfasts are so big that I'll probably meet someone new. But if I see the same man the following month I would not be able to recall his name nor he mine. With the smaller Men's Groups I will usually have everyone's first name down, but even if I know their last name and where they work I probably have no idea what challenges they're facing or who might be gifted in ways that could help me through my challenges.

Who in my group battles with pornography or anger? Who struggles with alcohol, drugs or gambling addictions? Who has committed adultery or struggles with sexual temptations? Who has been involved in an abortion and has never dealt with the psychological trauma that inevitably follows? Which of these guys has been through what I'm dealing with and could be a source of help and encouragement to me? What incredible stories are a part of the lives of the men sitting all around me that I will never hear or learn about?

A few years ago a friend and I started meeting each month and then it evolved so that we now meet each week for coffee early on Wednesday mornings. Through this relationship I have learned the value of having really strong relationships with other men; something called Spiritual Partnership. This friend, Rob Fischer, even wrote a book about this concept, **Comrades in Arms.** Today I maintain half a dozen of these relationships. Some of these men I meet with monthly and some weekly. They each know my strengths and my struggles and each one has my permission to tell me anything they feel needs to be said. They challenge me, encourage me, and freely offer me their wisdom. In short, these men are helping me write a better story. These men are helping me find purpose and meaning for my life. These men are helping me in some small way make the world a better place.

I'm confident that my story will be much better because of their influence in my life and hopefully they will benefit from me as well. These types of Spiritual Partnerships are very different from what men can achieve with their spouse and I have found that most men don't have even one such relationship.

Throughout my life, like everyone, I have had some very memorable events: my wedding, the birth of my children, the death of family members and close friends, other weddings, graduations, playing sports, school-yard fist-fights, hunting (killing things), those special moments with my wife and children (sometimes wanting to kill things), vacations, meeting famous people, real estate transactions (both good and bad) and the list could go on and on. All of our lives are full of these memories that will pass away when we do. As great as those memories are typically they are not transformational. Sure, in their own way these events have partly contributed to help me become who I am and what I am. But most of the "big" events in my life have not changed me.

My life is a journey consisting of hundreds of little stories that are constantly transforming me into becoming a better person. I believe that God will use not only the major problems I encounter, but He will also use seemingly minor interruptions to the regular routines of life to get my attention and speak to me if I'm willing to listen. I have been transformed through hundreds of books, movies, conversations (including those conversations with God, AKA Prayer) and the things that happen because "that's life."

These changes have been mostly incremental but a few have been significant. Maybe I'll have an experience and it moves my moral compass just a fraction of a degree towards true north. Or maybe I'll see a movie and it makes a huge change in the direction of my moral compass. One example of this is in 1977, the year I graduated from High School, the TV mini-series *Roots* came out. I would have never considered myself a racially bigoted person, I am white and my best friend in High School was black, but as I watched this series it became clear to me that I had been infected by the cultural norms of the area in which I grew up.

The Big Game is a book about stories. These stories are not necessarily big event stories but rather big impact stories. Each chapter is a short story that has in some way contributed to who I am. Some of these stories are funny and some are sad. Some are unbelievable but all are true to the best of my recollection (one possible exception might be the story involving a hawk, which I refuse to say is true or not on the grounds that if it were true it might be incriminating). In some stories I'm the hero, in some I'm the villain and in some my only role is as observer or third party. Some are glorious and some are embarrassing. Some are recent and others from a long time ago. Hopefully you'll be able to relate to most of these stories, but no doubt there will be some where you simply can't. In those cases glean the entertainment value and just move on.

Introduction

I think we all desire and strive to become better people. Hopefully I am becoming a better person, hopefully I have changed for the better and hopefully I will continue to grow, mature and become an even better person in the future. I am not the same person I was thirty years ago and I certainly hope I am not the same person ten or twenty years from now.

Even though these stories are meant to entertain there is a point to each one. Some of these stories deal with practical issues like money, business, relationships or family. But some of these stories deal with some of the cultural and social issues that we men typically don't want to talk about, things like sexual temptation, abortion and addictions.

It is my hope that as you read these stories you will see areas in your life that you have a good handle on. But you might also identify areas where you may need a little (or a lot of) help. It is also my hope that you will seek out at least one other man who will become a **Comrades in Arms** as my friend Rob explains in his book.

The Big Game is intended to be applicable for all men regardless of their race, religion or political views, but I'll tell you right up front that I am white, middle class, extremely conservative and a Christian. By "Christian" I mean someone that lives their life adhering to the teachings of Jesus Christ to the best of their ability and with the help of God. For some readers these are positive qualities but for others this information will plant a seed of skepticism. How you live your life and your view of God is none of my business. A few stories make mention of God but my intention for writing this book is not to convert anyone. However, in case God uses this book to stir your heart and show you that faith in Him will make you a better person then blame (or credit) Him.

Almost everything I have ever learned has come through the help of someone else, so this book is my attempt to give away some of the things that have so freely been given to me. My hope is that when you are finished reading this book you will look back and say you are a better, happier person and are now on your way to writing a better story.

CHAPTER 1

You Can't Buy Poverty

GROWING UP MY FAMILY WAS quite poor and buying food for our family of nine was very expensive. Some children seem to be oblivious to their family's economic status, but even at a very young age I knew we were poor. The topic of money and economic status will come up naturally in normal conversation and I can remember often saying that if someone would look in a dictionary for the definition of poverty they would find my family photo, except that the photo wouldn't be there because my family couldn't afford to have one taken.

When I was in the Fifth Grade my family moved from Sparta, Illinois to Colorado Springs, Colorado where Dad enrolled as a student in the Nazarene Bible College located there. Before this time my dad did not have any secondary education, I can remember him saying on many occasions, "Yeah, I went through college, I went in the front door and out the back door." Dad thought that college was a waste of time and would name several people he knew that went to college only to end up in some blue-collar job that didn't require a college education.

Dad had been a Minister in The Church of The Nazarene and at some point in the late sixties the Nazarene Church decided that all of their preachers needed a college degree. If my dad wanted to continue his career as a preacher he had to step away from the ministry and get a degree in theology. The Nazarene Bible College in Colorado Springs was established specifically for the purpose of offering a secondary education and a degree in theology to men and women who were beyond the normal college age.

Mom, Dad and seven kids made up our family of nine and attending college while trying to provide for our huge family meant some very tough times for Dad. He did this for a couple of years before dropping out and giving up his dream of being a preacher.

During this time, over a three-year span, I remember our family living in four different locations including a two-bedroom apartment. Four girls in one bedroom, three boys in the other and Mom and Dad sleeping on a hide a bed in the living room made things quite cozy to say the least. In this apartment building lived another family, the Cawveys. Mr. Cawvey was also attending the same college as my Dad.

My parents and the Cawvey family parents would go out twice a week to do what they called GP-ing, short for garbage picking. Back then the grocery stores were closed at night so they would bundle up and head out about 10pm to hit the dumpsters behind these closed grocery stores, getting get back home sometime around 2 or 3am. They would dig through the dumpsters to salvage whatever edible food they could: day-old bread; eggs in cartons where one or more eggs shells were broken; meat, milk, cheese and assorted dairy products that were beyond the expiration date; perfectly fine canned goods where the can had been dented.

Some nights wouldn't yield much of a windfall but other times they would hit the mother-lode. When they hit the mother-lode it was like Christmas at our house. Mom might scramble up a bunch of eggs and serve it with toast and milk at 3am and if it was a really good night we might have some bacon fried up to go along with it.

My wife freaks out when she finds a little mold on cheese or bread. I tell her to just cut it off and it will be fine, I've eaten plenty of it as a kid and it didn't seem to bother me. Her rebuttal is that the moldy bread and cheese might be the reason I'm so weird; she may be on to something there. I certainly wouldn't recommend eating moldy food if you don't have to.

Normal men fear things like death, public speaking, being beaten up, or asking a woman for a date, which can feel like being beaten up when you get her reply. But not me. My biggest fear in life was being poor. When I was in Junior High School I bought a poster that hung on my bedroom wall in all ten of the homes we lived in while I was in Junior High and High School. This poster also hung on a wall of my college dorm room when I lived in Chapman Hall, a men's dormitory at Northwest Nazarene University (NNU FKA NNC) in Nampa, Idaho. At that point in my life, those three years I lived in Chapman Hall were the longest stretch of time I had ever lived at the same address.

This poster simply said, "MONEY CAN'T BUY EVERYTHING...IT CAN'T BUY POVERTY." This statement was my motivation and worldview for many years. Sure, I tried to glamorize and spiritualize my desire for wealth by saying I intended to use my wealth to feed the poor, fund missionaries and build churches and homeless shelters all around the world. In my heart I truly intended to do exactly those things, but if the pursuit of wealth wasn't my god it was very close to being so.

I have always had entrepreneurial tendencies. I remember vividly, as a six-year old, being in the business of selling soda pop. I would buy a couple of cases of Coke from the service station across the street from our house, load the pop in a cooler filled with ice and head off pulling my cooler of pop in my little red wagon to a subdivision a few blocks away where new homes were being built. I would go from one construction site to another selling pop to the workers.

Back in those days pop was sold in bottles. To encourage recycling there was a two cent deposit required on every bottle and I would collect the two cent deposit from the construction workers at the time of sale. Even though I had collected the deposit, each evening I would return to the subdivision and pick up these same bottles.

A construction worker once questioned me about charging the deposit then coming back to pick up the bottles, implying that it was unfair. His co-worker told him to layoff and leave the kid alone. But even at six years of age I remember having the presence to tell this construction worker that I had to charge the deposit because I had no assurance that the bottles would be there when I came back that evening. That construction worker kept buying pop from me but never again left his bottles.

While in Junior High School I passed by a shopping mall on my walk to and from school. On my way home from school I would stop at a store in this mall and buy candy that I would sell to my friends at school for a modest profit. This little gig turned out to be a really sweet deal. I made money while going to school AND suddenly found myself becoming increasingly popular, something I had never before experienced. Not long into my new venture I was summoned to the Principal's office where he let me know that our Junior High School was his domain and that the laws of free market enterprise didn't apply there.

Being the compliant lad that I was...NOT! Operation candy sales was forced underground - the black market if you will. A second trip to the Principal's office included a threat to call my parents. So my candy selling business came to an end...at least for the time being.

I began playing the trumpet in Fifth Grade and continued through High School where I played my trumpet during my High School Graduation Ceremony. After that, I never touched the trumpet again. Been there, done that and bought the uniform. But that has nothing to do with this story.

In the same Junior High School where my candy career had just ended, the JHS Band decided to have a fundraiser. I don't remember what the fundraiser was for, but I do recall the Band Teacher driving a very nice new car later that year...just kidding. Anyway, the Band was to raise funds by - you guessed it - selling candy. It was starting to become very clear; the Principal wasn't just upset about me selling candy; he was upset because I was selling candy *on his turf.*

With these types of school fundraisers there are always prizes and incentives for those who reach certain sales goals and of course a big prize for the one who sells the most. When explaining the prizes and laying out the rules, the Band Teacher made some smart remark about my being ineligible to receive any prizes. He insinuated that my candy sales experience put me at an unfair advantage. But I knew what the teacher was really thinking; he knew I was a lock for the top prize.

All students were given twenty candy bars. Each candy bar sold for twenty-five cents. Those same candy bars sell for a buck today. The rules were simple: sell your twenty candy bars, turn in your five dollars and you would be given another twenty candy bars to sell. As long as you kept turning in your five bucks, proving your trustworthiness and ability, there was no limit to what you could do.

I'm guessing that you already know where this story is going. Care to take a guess as to how many candy bars I sold? Come on, try again, you're way off. You're still way off, want to try again? Alright, I won't continue to put you through this guessing game any longer. The number of candy bars I sold for my Junior High School Band Fundraiser was……….. Drum-roll please……………zero. Yes, that's right, zero.

I think it would be safe to say that no one in history has ever sold zero candy bars in their school fundraiser. It is inconceivable that there is any kid on this planet who couldn't manage at least a few sales. While I didn't sell a single candy bar, the events surrounding this candy bar fundraiser would significantly impact my life and play a huge role in who and what I was to become.

After school on the day that the fundraiser began I grabbed my books and my bag of twenty candy bars and headed over to the gym to play basketball. Lockers were not assigned in the locker-room so we'd bring our own lock, find an empty locker, shove our clothes and junk in the locker, put our lock on it and head off to play ball. After playing basketball I came back into the locker-room and when I opened my locker my clothes were all there but my bag of twenty candy bars was gone.

I went and found the coach and told him what had happened. The coach came over to my locker and in a matter-of-fact manner says, "Oh yea, this locker doesn't work!" He demonstrated by putting my lock back on the locker door then took hold of my lock and gave it a firm jerk and the locker door popped right open. "But what about my candy bars?" I cried pathetically. Talking over his shoulder as he walked away, "You gotta see the Principal about that." "Oh great," I thought, the last thing I wanted was another trip to the Principal's office. We weren't exactly best buds at this point.

Now I was always one to have some money around. But on this particular day in my life, except for my coin collection I had less than a dollar to my name. I remember at home that night telling my parents what had happened and asking them if I could borrow five dollars. I also remember my father telling me he would be happy to lend me five dollars but he just didn't have it. I had always kind of known we were poor but this was the first time I realized just how poor we really were and what that actually meant in a bigger picture sort of way.

My Band Teacher and the Principal were surprisingly understanding. I promised that I would do whatever I needed to do to earn the money to pay off my five dollar debt for the candy bars. But rules are rules and I was not issued any more candy bars for the duration of the fundraiser.

I indeed earned the money to pay my debt but it wasn't until after the allotted time for the fundraiser had ended. When I went to pay my debt I was told that they had caught the thief and that they had required payment from him. I truly do not know if they indeed caught the thief and whether or not the thief paid for his crime but my suspicion is that they just didn't feel right about taking five dollars from this poor kid.

While I can look back and say that this experience taught me some great lessons about honoring your commitments, mercy and forgiveness, I also came away from this experience with an unhealthy view of money and independence. That night, after I had asked to borrow five dollars from my parents, I went off by myself and made a vow that I would never be poor again. I also vowed that I would never again need anyone for anything and I especially never again wanted to be in a position where I needed to ask anyone for money.

In the correct application, being independent and self-motivated are healthy characteristics. But taken to extreme and attempted for several years, my vow for independence proved futile. I had to be reminded that God is God and I am not. If I was going to live a happy, productive and purposeful life, I could not do it without the help of God, family and friends.

Whenever I hear someone say that money changes people I disagree with them. I do not believe that money, fame or power changes anyone. I believe it *reveals* them. True integrity, generosity and good character are never lost when someone comes into money, fame or power. These things only reveal either that one truly has good character or that one never really had it to begin with.

If someone were to ask me what are the most important things in my life today my response would be as follows (my seven Fs):

1) Faith
2) Freedom
3) Family
4) Friends
5) Fitness
6) Finances
7) Fun

Today my wife and I live on a fraction of what I used to make and I can honestly say that I'm just as happy as I have ever been.

REFLECTION

1) What part of Perry's story did you identify with the most?

_____

_____

_____

_____

_____

2) How would you describe your view of money?

_____

_____

_____

_____

_____

3) What negative effects of materialism have you seen or experienced?_____

_____

_____

_____

_____

4) Wealthy is a relative term. But in what ways would you say you are wealthy? _____

_____

_____

_____

_____

5) What responsibility does wealth bring with it? _____

_____

_____

_____

_____

6) Be completely honest with yourself and list the most important things in your life. Where does money fall on your list?

_____

_____

_____

_____

_____

CHAPTER 2

The Hawk and the Pitchfork

WE LIVE ON A SMALL farm where we have a few chickens. Well Okay, we have A LOT of chickens. Let me give you an idea just how many chickens we have. One evening we had both of our daughters and their families out for dinner. What was supposed to be a nice relaxing time to visit with all the family turned into a chicken intervention for Dad (me). Both of my son-in-laws were wise enough to keep their opinions to themselves, but my wife and daughters were very expressive in their opinion that we had "too many chickens." So I carefully laid out the logic behind the need to have so many chickens.

We have an egg incubator and it takes twenty-one days of incubation for a chicken egg to hatch. Each month I put about four dozen eggs in the incubator with the hope of hatching an average of thirty healthy chicks. Our collective families go through (eat) fifteen chickens per month. Since only half of our chicks will be cockerels (boys) and destined to have their heads removed from their necks when they mature, we need thirty healthy chicks each month just to produce the chickens our families need for eating. The other half of the chicks will be pullets (girls) that will eventually grow up to lay eggs, so we want to keep their heads attached to their necks. Once a pullet reaches maturity and is not needed for our egg production, we can easily sell it to some other fool who will also unwittingly create some family conflict.

It takes approximately five months for a chick to grow to maturity. During that time, the cockerels become roosters and the pullets become hens. If we start with thirty chicks each month, the five-month-chicken-raising process will create a chick-to-chicken pipeline of 150 chicks in the various stages of development. In addition to the 150 chicks in the pipeline, roosters and hens are needed for the production of eggs which are sold, eaten, or incubated.

Okay, enough of *"Chickens for Dummies."* Even after I clearly spelled out the chicken operational needs, my wife and daughters would have none of it. They still insisted that we had "too many chickens." When I asked them how many chickens they thought we should have they offered a variety of opinions on the optimum number. But none of them could provide any sort of rationale as to why they chose their particular number; they offered numbers that "just sounded good."

I finally said to my wife, "OK, you're right, we have too many chickens. You show me which ones you'd like me to get rid of and I'll take care of them tomorrow." Yes, it was a low blow; I know how much my wife detests the process of me removing the chickens' heads from their necks. My wonderful wife gave me her, "You are such an idiot" look and there the intervention ended.

Chickens are amazing creatures. We allow our chickens to "free range." This means they have the freedom to go anywhere on our six-acre farm except for places we don't want them, like the front porch and the garden. Chickens not only provide meat and eggs, but because we allow them to free range, our chickens serve as a garbage disposal, lawnmower, lawn fertilizer and insect removal for the entire farm. A friend of mine describes chickens as "God's gift to man."

But I call chickens "pets with a purpose." You see, dogs and cats just lie around only getting up occasionally to eat and poop. Chickens not only provide all of the benefits just mentioned but they are cheaper to buy, cheaper to feed, don't require walking, don't require trips to the vet, don't care to ride in your car or the back of your pickup, and poop in small enough quantities that it doesn't require cleanup of the yard.

I admit that chickens do have their downside. There is nothing like shoveling out the chicken coop every couple of weeks to remind me that in the grand scheme of things I just ain't all that important. My wife calls it God's way of keeping me humble. Another downside to chickens is that you can't just drop them off at the in-laws if you want to leave town for a few days. We chicken folk need to have friends and neighbors who know our routine. These friends and neighbors are generally happy to lend a hand as long as it doesn't include the previously mentioned downside as they are already quite humble enough.

But the greatest benefit to having chickens over dogs or cats is the entertainment value. No television needed here. I can, and do, sit and watch our chickens for hours. From time to time my wife and I will haul a couple of lawn chairs out to the chicken run and just sit there drinking iced tea while watching the chickens scratch, peck and do those curious things that chickens do. It's not that we are weird; anyone with chickens will tell you the same thing. Dogs or cats just don't provide the same entertainment value.

In spite of my earlier comments about the benefits of having chickens rather than dogs or cats for pets, there is one clear disadvantage. Chickens reside pretty low on the food chain. I agree with my friend that chickens are indeed God's gift to man, but my experience has led me to believe that they are also God's gift to a number of His other wonderful creatures. Chickens seem to also be God's gift to coyotes, hawks, owls, skunks and most of all, the neighbor's dog.

One Friday afternoon I had to leave the farm for a meeting. Everything was fine at home and I knew my wife would be coming home from work in a matter of minutes. So, thinking that my wife would appreciate the gesture, I left the gate open so she wouldn't have to get out of her car to open it. In those few minutes between my departure and her arrival something awful happened. My poor wife drove up to our house only to find thirteen dead chickens strewn throughout the yard, the work of a neighbor's dog. It was totally my fault for leaving the gate open. I felt worse for her finding this carnage than I felt over the loss of the chickens.

While we let our mature chickens free range during the day, we lock our chickens in two separate coops every night to minimize our chicken losses to predators. As the sun sets the chickens naturally start heading into their coops where they will roost for the night. Generally, within fifteen or twenty minutes, all will be safely inside their coops. Sometimes we will wait until about twenty minutes after sunset and just go out to close and latch the coop doors. Other times we will embrace the entertainment value and go out a few minutes early to watch the chickens as they go through their nightly rituals. Enjoying the chickens' entertainment value was exactly what I was doing on this memorable autumn evening.

I had gone outside right at sunset and to my surprise all of the chickens in our larger coop were already inside. All I had to do was to shut and latch the door. Hoping that our smaller coop would be just as easy I walked over to it but found that almost all of the forty-plus chickens were still scratching around and taking their sweet ole time about heading indoors. I really didn't care. I leaned against a fence-post for almost half an hour and enjoyed watching the playful antics of our chickens as one by one they headed into the coop.

When there were only eight of these chickens remaining outside and it was starting to get dark, suddenly out of nowhere an enormous hawk landed on top of a chicken about thirty feet away from me. I was so startled by the hawk that I let out an instinctive "Ahhhhhh!" shout. I'd like to think that my shout was to protect the chicken and chase away the hawk, but in all honesty my shout was merely my response to having the crap scared out of me.

Even after my shout this enormous hawk, holding the chicken in its talons, just stood there glaring at me as if to say, "I've got your chicken and there ain't a darn thing you can do about it." At this point in the story I'll insert that the night ended well for the chicken but not so well for the hawk. You are free to use your imagination to make whatever conclusions you wish, but I will offer a couple of possible scenarios as to what I meant when I said that the night did not end so well for the hawk. The second of these possible scenarios is so outrageously absurd that it could not possibly be true.

The first possible scenario is that the hawk finally came to its senses and flew away without any dinner. For those of you who might be sensitive animal-lover types, sensitive nature-lover types, or anyone involved in law enforcement this first scenario is actually what happened so you can ignore the other, absurd and totally fabricated, second possible scenario. You need not read any further in this chapter and may move on to the next. For those not quite convinced you may read on.

Before getting into the second scenario (the scenario which is a total fabrication and so utterly impossible that it is absurd to even suggest) I need to point out something. I have heard rumors of farmers and ranchers that use a predator management plan commonly referred to as the Three S's of Predator Management: Shoot, Shovel and Shut-up. They also adhere to the belief that the "Shoot" portion of their Predator Management Plan can be accomplished through some other means. When this happens, the other two parts, "Shovel and Shut-up," are to remain in place. Now I personally would never behave in this manner because it is illegal and would involve large, punitive fines for those who do.

So back to a second possible scenario which is just one of dozens of possible scenarios. I'm not saying this happened and I'm not saying it didn't, here you have the opportunity to use your imagination, maybe even dream up a scenario of your own. OK, where were we… Even after my shout this enormous hawk, holding the chicken in its talons, just stood there glaring at me as if to say, "I've got your chicken and there ain't a darn thing you can do about it." The night ended well for the chicken but not so well for the hawk.

Just maybe there was a pitchfork leaning against the chicken coop and just maybe I grabbed the pitchfork and flung it in the direction of the huge, chicken-stealing hawk. And just maybe my pitchfork hurling skills were a bit rusty and just maybe, because of the adrenaline rushing through my veins, my throw went a bit too high. Just maybe, at the exact moment of my pitchfork hurl, the hawk realized that he was not in a good situation and that this might be a good time to make an exit. Just maybe the hawk made one gigantic leap away from me before launching into flight. Just maybe as the hawk took off it intersected the flight path of the errantly thrown pitchfork and just maybe the hawk was knocked to the ground, dazed by its in-flight encounter with a pitchfork handle.

Just maybe I ran up to the hawk and grabbed its leg before it could come to his senses. Just maybe I refused to let go of the hawk's leg as it relentlessly pounded me up with his wings in his attempt to escape. Just maybe I was able to wrestle him to the ground and just maybe I was able to grab his second leg and bring the beast under my control. Holding the hawk by its legs, just maybe I put my foot on the hawk's neck applying all the pressure I could as he continued to pummel me with his wings. Just maybe this pressure was continuously applied until the hawk became motionless.

Just maybe I went to my pickup and got a flashlight out of the glovebox and just maybe I went to the tool shed and pulled a shovel off of the wall. Just maybe I would be smart enough to shut-up and never, never, never tell a soul about the event involving the hawk and the pitchfork.

REFLECTION

1) What part of Perry's story did you identify with the most?

_____

_____

_____

_____

_____

2) How are disagreements handled in your home?

_____

_____

_____

_____

_____

3) To what extent is it a man's responsibility to protect his family and property?

_____

_____

_____

_____

_____

4) How would you describe courage?

_____

_____

_____

_____

_____

5) To what extent would you describe yourself as being a courageous person?

_____

_____

_____

_____

_____

6) In what ways could you live more courageously?

_____

_____

_____

_____

_____

CHAPTER 3

Stengel's Gun Shop

MY FAMILY MOVED FROM SPARTA, Illinois to Colorado Springs, Colorado when I was ten years old and we lived in Colorado for the next five years. When I was fifteen my family moved back to Illinois to a very small town by the name of Barry where we lived for only about a year. While living in Barry these few months I turned sixteen and obtained my driver's license. But shortly after getting my Illinois driver's license my family moved back to Colorado, just outside another small town named Hotchkiss.

A huge benefit to living in Colorado is the big game hunting. I was proud of the fact that at the age of ten I had been one of the very first persons to complete the Colorado Hunter Safety Course. I began big game hunting at age fourteen. Except for the year I was fifteen and living in Illinois, I went big-game hunting most of the thirty-plus years I lived in Colorado. When we lived in Illinois we hunted rabbits and squirrels but now that we were back in Colorado I was very excited to once again be hunting the big stuff like deer, elk and bear.

I killed my first deer when I was sixteen and my first elk at seventeen. Overall I'd guess that I have bagged around thirty-five elk and fifty or so deer. A few of these animals would make any hunter proud.

About four miles west of Hotchkiss and just a short ways from our house was a very small gun shop on Highway 92 known as Stengel's Gun Shop. Old Man Stengel had this gun shop in his basement where he had an outside entrance. He also had a fantastic shooting range out behind the gun shop. The locals would buy guns, ammunition, hunting licenses and some of the more common hunting accessories such as game bags, knives, scopes, hunting vests, hats and gloves. It was also a great place to "sight" your rifle and get in a little shooting practice before hunting season opened.

Stengel's was a great little gun shop but just as much as it was a gun shop it was also a hang-out for the locals to stop by and shoot the breeze with Ole Man Stengel. Stengel was extremely knowledgeable, at least from a sixteen-year-old's perspective. He seemed to know everything anyone needed to know about guns or hunting. One day in late September or early October I drove over to Stengel's in my green '61 Chevy Apache 10 pickup with the intent of buying a Colorado resident "sportsman's license." This was a combination license for deer, elk, bear and mountain lion.

Important to this story is knowing that in Colorado there are "resident" licenses and "non-resident" licenses. The only difference is that a "non-resident" license has an additional cost of several hundred dollars; something this sixteen-year-old could not afford. It is also important to note that to obtain a "resident" hunting license the hunter had to be a Colorado resident for six months. Colorado also required that new residents change their out-of-state driver's license to a Colorado license within three months of moving into the state. At the time of this particular event my family had only been back in Colorado for four months. Also at this time, I had not yet exchanged my Illinois driver's license for a Colorado one.

I parked my pickup and went inside Stengel's where Ole Man Stengel was chewing the fat with some other fellow. As I walked in Stengel looked up from his conversation and asked, "How can I help you young man?"

"I'd like to buy a sportsman's license," I replied.

Stengel reached under the counter and pulled out this little booklet of licenses and handed it to me.

"Fill this out and be sure to press hard because we have to be able to read all three copies," he instructed me.

Stengel went back to his conversation with the other guy and I started filling out the paperwork for the license. I came to the question, "Are you a Colorado resident?" to which I checked "yes." To the next question, "If a resident, how long have you lived in Colorado?" I answered, "five years and four months." In my mind this answer was completely accurate; I simply ignored the piece of information involving the few months when I lived in Illinois. The next question on the application was "Driver's license number?" which I left blank. I left this question blank because I had not yet transferred my Illinois driver's license to a Colorado Driver's License and to list my Illinois license number might draw questions about my status as a "resident."

I finished the paperwork and handed the booklet back to Stengel. He looked it over and noticed that I had left "Driver's license number" blank.

"What's your driver's license number?" he asked.

"I don't have one," I replied, of course thinking that I don't have a Colorado driver's license.

"Wasn't that you who drove up in that Chevy pickup out there?" he asks.

"Yes sir," I said.

Stengel stood up from leaning on the counter, took a deep breath and said,

"Son, I'd like to introduce you to Mr. So-and-So, he is one of our fine public servants with the Colorado Highway Patrol."

I must have turned twenty shades of red because I knew I was going to jail. The word "BUSTED" cannot even begin to describe how I felt. Once I gained my composure I explained that I indeed had a driver's license from Illinois, pulling it out of my wallet to prove it and I also explained my rationale for claiming five plus years of residency. Stengel and the off-duty Highway Patrol Officer had the biggest laugh at my expense. Stengel indeed sold me the desired hunting license as the officer warned me to immediately transfer my driver's license to Colorado.

With my hunting license in hand I could not get out of that gun shop fast enough. If that was where this story had ended it would have never been such a memorable event or included in this book. As I stated earlier, Stengel's was a local hangout for guys to come in and shoot the breeze with ole man Stengel. Stengel now had a funny story that he felt compelled to share with everyone that stopped in to chat, which included my dad and almost every other man in the county.

For months I endured listening to Dad tell this story to family and friends over and over. He told this story with so much flare and enthusiasm that those hearing it for the first time were under the impression that he had been there and witnessed the incident first-hand. It wasn't just Dad; it seemed to be the whole stinking county making wise-cracks about it. No serious hunter could avoid Stengel's, so I had to relive this event each time I returned to his shop, or even drove past it, which was pretty much every day.

I admit that I still have a bit of rebel in me when it comes to laws I think are ridiculous, or areas where I believe our government has over-stepped its Constitutional authority. But beyond that I'm pretty much a "by the rules" kind of a guy. I can't help but think this incident played a huge role in my becoming that way.

REFLECTION

1) What part of Perry's story did you identify with the most?

_____

_____

_____

_____

_____

2) In what way is telling "a little white lie" different from telling any other lie?

_____

_____

_____

_____

_____

3) Describe a situation when telling a lie would not be considered wrong. _____

_____

_____

_____

_____

4) To what extent would withholding information to intentionally give someone a wrong impression be considered lying?

_____

_____

_____

_____

_____

5) In what ways have you deceived others?

_____

_____

_____

_____

_____

6) When it comes to being a man of your word, how do you think others would describe you?

_____

_____

_____

_____

_____

7) In what ways or areas of your life do you need to become more honest?

_____

_____

_____

_____

_____

CHAPTER 4

Fishing in Alaska

I AM TERRIBLE WHEN IT COMES to fishing. I grew up in Colorado where we naturally were hunters. Game was abundant and except for mountain reservoirs, large bodies of water do not exist. We depended on hunting for our food and fishing simply couldn't provide the food we needed.

Not only could fishing not provide the food we needed but most of my fishing experiences were BORING. For me fishing meant putting a worm on my hook, casting my line into the water, sitting in a lawn chair and staring at my pole for hours on end while praying for a fish to bite. I tried stream fishing a few times but the result ended up being just another flavor of the same torture; a lot of time spent with very little to show for it. There are men out there that are awesome fishermen; I'm just not one of them.

A couple of my friends had small boats and we would fish by "trolling." When trolling we definitely caught more and bigger fish, but in the end it still meant sitting on my butt all day waiting for a fish to take my bait. The only difference is that with trolling the bait was moving, following us behind the boat. I have a few memorable fishing experiences during my years in Colorado. These times are memorable because of the *size* of fish I caught or because of the *number* of the fish I caught. When fishing in Colorado a nice-sized fish might run a pound or two and on a couple of occasions the fish I caught may have even tipped the scales in the four-pound range.

Whenever a friend would call me to invite me to go fishing, sure, I would go. And if we were trolling I might even be a little excited about going. But fishing was an activity that I would rarely, if ever, initiate. Fishing was something I never had a passion for. This all changed. What caused this change? I moved to Alaska.

When I arrived in Alaska it was the dead of winter and I brought with me the anti-fishing bias that had served me well for years. The summer following my arrival I was invited to go halibut fishing as a guest. My host was the owner of a mortgage company where my real estate company sent a great deal of loan business. Basically, the owner of this mortgage company was being really nice to me because my company referred a lot of business to him and made him a great deal of money.

I gladly accepted the halibut fishing offer without having the slightest clue what I was about to get into. All I was told was to dress warm and bring rain gear; everything else would be provided. I knew we would be fishing for halibut, but I had never before even seen a halibut much less caught one. As I recall, the boat was cozy but big enough to comfortably accommodate four fishermen plus a skipper and a deck hand.

Before heading out, there was a bit of a discussion about some commonly held superstition involving bananas on fishing vessels. The skipper asked if anyone had any bananas and I admitted that I had snagged one from the continental breakfast at the hotel. The skipper insisted that I discard it. There was even some discussion about leaving me on shore because I had eaten a banana the previous day and they feared that some of that banana might still remain within me. I may have gone a bit *overboard* in my response to their banana superstition.

No reason was offered for the "no bananas" rule. The skipper had the attitude, "My boat, my rule, no bananas, and no discussion." Hey, it was his boat so I graciously tossed my banana into the ocean. I seemed to be the only person unaware of the rule, but I've since learned that the rule is fairly universal throughout Alaska. For anyone unfamiliar with the drill this is truly an unbelievable superstition. But if you ever go fishing in Alaska DO NOT take along any bananas…these people are insane about their "no bananas" rule.

Leaving the banana behind, we took off from shore and traveled out into the ocean for about an hour before dropping anchor. The deck hand "rigged up" a pole, baited the hook with a six inch hooligan fish, dropped the line into the water and handed me the pole. "If you feel something just let 'em take it and reel 'em in when ya know they're hooked," he told me.

"Got it," I replied while hoping not to embarrass myself any further after the banana episode.

I don't think three minutes had gone by before my pole started doing the herky-jerky and I knew I had something on the line. I reeled in this "huge" five pound fish which had to be, up to this point in my life, the biggest fish I had ever caught. I was sooo proud. "Is it a halibut?" I asked.

Without hesitation and in one smooth motion the deck hand ripped the fish off of my line, placed the fish on the boat workbench with his left hand, grabbed a meat cleaver with his right hand and chopped my prized trophy fish in half while saying, "Nope, it's a cod. But that's okay, now we have some bait." He then re-baited my hook with half of my fish and told me to let my line down, all the way to the bottom.

I stood there shaking my head and in shock, trying to comprehend what had just happened. This deckhand...this kid...had just taken the *biggest fish* I had ever caught and used it for *bait!* Can you feel my pain? But I quickly realized that if my fish was being used for bait much larger fish were probably not far behind. Feeling that I needed to conceal my shock and to get in the last word I calmly said, "So that's what you use for bait...wouldn't a banana have worked just as well?" I'm not a great swimmer so that is where the banana conversation ended.

I may have started the day by having to chuck my banana but the day ended very well. We filled our limit of halibut and I had a couple of sixty pounders and a few measly five pound cod to my credit.

In another episode of Alaska fishing I received a call from a friend of mine named Dean. He called to tell me that his family and two other families from church were heading to Kenai to go "dipnetting." He asked if our family would like to join them. This was on a Friday afternoon and would involve driving down to Kenai that evening and spending the night. All of the other families had tents and camping gear, but we were new to Alaska and had sold all of our camping equipment in a garage sale before moving from Colorado.

I called all five Kenai hotels with no luck; due to the salmon runs all of the hotels were full. On my fifth and final call I had just been told that they had no vacancy. But just as I was about to hang up the operator jumped back in to tell me that just as we were speaking she had received a cancellation and now had a room available. I grabbed the room. I called Dean back and told him to count us in and to get some idea as to what to expect from this thing he called dipnetting. In short he told me that all we needed was a dipnet, waders and our fishing license.

So that you have a better idea as to what dipnetting is about here are a few important details:

1) Each year in Alaska hundreds of thousands of salmon come out of the ocean in what are called "salmon runs" as they swim up the many rivers towards spawning waters.

2) Salmon spawning happens throughout the many rivers dumping into the ocean waters along the Alaska coast. But the Kenai River in Kenai, Alaska is probably the most popular due to its proximity to the more populated areas of the state.

3) Only Alaskan residents are permitted to dipnet.

4) Most of the salmon that are caught while dipnetting are sockeye salmon also known to Alaskans as "red salmon."

5) Most sockeye salmon caught by dipnetting are fully mature and headed to spawning waters where they would otherwise spawn and die.

6) Sockeye Salmon caught dipnetting will generally weigh six to seven pounds.

7) Most dipnets are nets that are five feet in diameter at the end of a pole twelve to twenty feet in length.

There is no "personal bubble" while dipnetting. Commonly called "combat fishing," people stand shoulder-to-shoulder in frigid glacial waters while hanging on to their dipnetting poles as if their life depended on it, which it often does. When salmon swim into their net the dipnetter will drag their net out of the water and whack the fish on the top of the head with a wooden fish whacker. The fish whacker looks like a miniature baseball bat and is used to kill the fish and keep it from flopping all over the place including back into the water. After successfully landing a salmon the dipnetter will push his net back out into the water to do it all over again. The number of fish you can catch via dipnetting is determined by the number of people in your household; a family of five would be allowed to catch sixty-five salmon in this manner.

We arrived at the Kenai River dipnetting area at about 9:30pm. It was mid-July and sunset in Kenai this time of year is around 11:30pm. Sunrise is around 5:00am so we knew that it was not going to get dark; we could dipnet as long as we wanted. The line of cars vying to enter the fishing area was about a quarter mile long, but the good news was that it was late enough in the day that there were just as many cars leaving as there were arriving.

After entering the dipnetting area the road tees. Turning right takes visitors to the parking area and turning left takes visitors down a one-car lane that is three to four hundred yards long. At the end of this lane there is a turnaround where people and gear are dropped off and picked up. This one-car lane was absolutely CRAZY. With traffic trying to go both directions on the one-car lane and with a turnaround area at the end of the lane that was packed with vehicles being loaded and unloaded, this lane was as close to being gridlocked as is possible without actually being so.

As I drove into this crazy, congested, disorganized mess I sensed that I was beginning to develop a very bad attitude, my blood pressure began to rise and my patience was waning. Notwithstanding my attitude and the crazy traffic situation in which I found myself, it somehow all seemed to work.

We finally made our way to the drop-off area and I readily admit that I was still sporting a bad attitude. I was fully aware that after dropping off my wife, son and gear I had to negotiate my way back up the lane. I then had the impossible task of finding a parking spot then return on foot to where I had dumped the family and gear. What had I gotten myself roped into I wondered?

I was fortunate enough to quickly find a parking spot and I parked the pickup. At this point I had yet to see the Kenai River where we would be dipnetting. The river and the lane ran parallel to each other and were separated by an earthen levy. I made my way back to the drop-off zone and headed up the path over the levy. As I came to the top of the levy I saw for the first time what dipnetting was all about and from where I was standing it wasn't pretty. As I have stated earlier I had always considered fishing to be boring, but the solitude is what had made fishing bearable for me in the past. There would be no solitude here and with that I felt my bad attitude go from bad to really bad.

There were hundreds of tents lining both sides of the mouth of the Kenai River. There weren't just dozens or even hundreds of people standing in the cold waters of the river, there were thousands of people. There was a line of people on both sides of the river standing shoulder-to-shoulder in waist deep water with their five-foot diameter nets at the end of their ten to twenty foot poles for as far as I could see.

The three families that we came with were busy setting up their tents and campsites when my friend Dean suggested that I walk down to the river and see what was happening. He saw that my net was only a small net used for landing fish caught from a boat and offered me the use of his dipnet while he set up camp. I put on my hip, that's right, *hip* waders and made my way out to the combat fishing line knowing that this entire ordeal was a complete waste of time.

My really bad attitude got even worse when I realized that everyone else along the combat fishing line was wearing chest waders when all I had was hip waders; I couldn't even get out to the fishing line. I remember rolling my eyes and feeling disgusted as I waded out as far as I dared and put my borrowed net in water that was only a few feet beyond the line of fisherman. I was embarrassed to be there.

At this point in my life I was as ill-prepared and as dipnetting-ignorant as anyone could possibly be. The one thing that I did know was how to use a whacker. But I had such a bad attitude and was so pessimistic about the prospects of landing a fish that I didn't bother bringing my whacker out to the water with me. I had intentionally left my whacker with my other gear back where our friends' camps were being set up, about a hundred yards from the river.

I settled into my dipnetting position as best I could. I had been there for less than a minute when I saw someone near me pull in a sockeye salmon. This was the first encouraging sign I had seen so I started asking questions of another dipnetter standing near me. "How will I know if there's a fish in my net?" I asked.

"Oh, you'll know," he said.

I had been standing in the water for less than five minutes and I immediately came to life when all of the sudden my pole started jerking my arms relentlessly. A salmon had found its way into my net. I dragged the fish to the beach and was staring at this seven pound sockeye wondering how I could have been so stupid to leave my whacker in the camping area. Another fisherman saw me chasing and trying to subdue this huge salmon as it flopped all over the beach. I think he took pity on me because he loaned me his whacker and I finished off the magnificent fish. I hurried back to the camping area to fetch my whacker and a cooler in which to keep the fish until I could clean it later.

Talk about an attitude adjustment; in about sixty seconds I had gone from having a really bad attitude to being as giddy as a child at Christmas.

I dipnetted for another hour and landed six more salmon. Since I had to borrow a dipnet and others from our group were anxious to get started, my wife, son and I left around midnight to check into our hotel. I cleaned our seven salmon in the hotel kitchenette which was probably not the most thoughtful thing I've ever done. I finally fell into bed around 1am thinking that it had been a good day.

The next morning we slept in a bit and took our time getting around. We stopped at McDonald's for breakfast then headed back to the river. I dropped my son and wife off at the drop-off zone and went to park the pickup. As I was walking down the lane, heading back towards the drop-off area, I saw my wife about a hundred yards away hollering something at me and motioning that I should hurry. With all the commotion she was making I was sure that someone had drowned so I ran towards her as fast as I could. "You won't believe how many fish everyone is catching. You gotta get down there and get a net in the water," She said.

"Well I'm thrilled that everyone is still alive…I'll get right on that DEAR," I replied with what little breath I had remaining. It was about 10:30am when I started dipnetting on this second and final day of our trip.

By 3:30pm my wife and I had landed thirty-five salmon and stopped only because we were confident that we had all that we needed. The other guys and I spent the next two hours cleaning and filleting the 250 salmon that the four families had collectively harvested. What had started out to be a most dreaded outing turned out to be one of my most memorable events of the ten years I lived in Alaska. From that day on dipnetting became a much-anticipated annual event.

While dipnetting a few years later my wife landed a twenty-eight pound King salmon, I was impressed. Not to be outdone, my son-in-law dipnetted a forty-three pound King the following day. During our ten years in Alaska I caught my share of King salmon but never one while dipnetting. Fishing in Alaska has spoiled me a bit; lake or stream fishing anywhere else just isn't quite the same as what I have experienced there. But I have decided that any fishing experience can be an enjoyable one if done without my bad attitude.

REFLECTION

1) What part of Perry's story did you identify with the most?

_____

_____

_____

_____

_____

2) What has been your greatest source of disappointment?

_____

_____

_____

_____

_____

3) To what extend would you say your disappointments are tied to your expectations?

_____

_____

_____

_____

_____

4) In what ways does your attitude contribute to your anger?

_____

_____

_____

_____

_____

5) What negative effects of anger have you seen or experienced in yourself or others?

_____

_____

_____

_____

_____

6) What situations have you recognize that tend to trigger your anger? _____

_____

_____

_____

_____

7) What can you intentionally do to become a man who is slow to become angry? _____

_____

_____

_____

_____

CHAPTER 5

When Ya Gotta Go

IT WAS SEPTEMBER IN THE year 2000. I was only forty-one years old and our oldest daughter, Christy had graduated from High School in May earlier that year. Rather than going straight into college she decided that she would take off a couple of years to participate in a youth program called Route 24/7, which was offered through New Life Church in Colorado Springs. Christy had already moved to Colorado Springs but had learned that the accommodations she had been provided were a bit lacking. Her housing was with a young single woman who provided a room for Christy but had no furniture for the room.

To help her out my wife and I loaded some of Christy's furniture and together with Christy's younger brother made the five-hour drive from our home in Grand Junction to Colorado Springs. Traveling to Colorado Springs was fairly routine; some of our life-long closest friends, Carl & Jennie lived there and we were looking forward to staying at their home and spending some time with them.

My wife, Sue and Christy had some shopping to do, so I was given the address and a key to the apartment where Christy was staying.

Our son stayed with me. I found the apartment and thought to myself, "Great…Why can't people live on the ground level?" I had a pickup load of furniture that had to be hauled up a long, narrow flight of stairs and my son wasn't yet big enough to give me any real help. I psyched myself up with my John Wayne pep talk which went something like, "Hey, I'm Superman…I can do this…suck it up, quit your whining and deal with it like a man." Half an hour later I was all done, in my pickup and headed back towards our friends' home.

On the way back to my friend's house I decided to stop and fill my pickup with gas. I pulled into the gas station, got out of the pickup, shoved the nozzle into the fuel tank and just as I leaned over to pick up the window washing squeegee I felt a snap in my lower back.

Throughout my High School and College years I worked in the family construction business, mostly doing very physical work like hanging and finishing sheet-rock. I had also been very active playing sports; even then at age forty-one I was still playing city league softball and basketball. Years of abusing my back combined with the fact that I was forty pounds overweight finally caught up with me in that moment.

The pain was excruciating. It took every ounce of strength I could muster to remove the fuel nozzle and crawl back into the pickup. As I drove the fifteen minutes to our friend's house I used every driving trick in the book to keep from having to lift my leg to engage the clutch or brake.

It seemed like an eternity but I finally arrived at our friends' house and told our son, "Daddy is hurting really bad. Go in the house and get some help." Apparently I did not adequately communicate the gravity of the situation to my son. I sat in the pickup, unable to move for what seemed like hours; in reality it was probably only twenty minutes. Finally my friend Carl came looking for me; he had seen our son go through the house and started wondering where I was. Carl went across the street to get a neighbor and the two of them assisted me into the house. Once inside, I felt only minimal pain as long as I remained stretched out on the floor and did not try to move. But any movement created unbearable pain.

My friend Carl was a paramedic with the Colorado Springs Fire Department and after several hours of seeing no improvement, he advised that I be transported to the hospital. Carl called the Fire Station where he worked and the entire squad showed up with a firetruck, ambulance and the whole shebang. They drove me to the hospital where I was admitted and had my very first experience as a hospital patient. There I spent the night doped up on pain-killers and muscle-relaxers. The next morning, still in a fog but at least able to move, my wife drove us home while I slept the entire five-hour trip.

If that was all there was to this story I doubt I would bother to tell it. As Paul Harvey used to say, "And now, the rest of the story."

When the firemen showed up I had been lying on our friends' living-room floor for several hours. Just as these firemen were about to put me on a stretcher I insisted that some other business needed to be attended to first – I needed to pee. And if I didn't pee and pee real soon one of these nice firemen would be cleaning up a mess that was about to be all over their shiny new stretcher and their ambulance floor. When put in these terms the firemen seemed to agree that helping me pee was not a bad idea.

Our friend Jennie brought us a flower vase and then she left the room, for that I was thankful. Four firemen gathered around me, bearing my weight and lifting me to my knees. From this position I was high enough to get my pants open and commence the discharge. It was a good thing that Jennie brought us such a large vase because anything smaller would have been insufficient to handle it all. I don't think Jennie was very sentimental about that vase; after emptying it she promptly threw it away.

REFLECTION

1) What part of Perry's story did you identify with the most?

_____

_____

_____

_____

_____

2) How would you describe your attitude towards physical fitness?

_____

_____

_____

_____

_____

3) Describe your most physically painful experience.

_____

_____

_____

_____

_____

4) Describe your most emotionally painful experience.

_____

_____

_____

_____

_____

5) How have you dealt with your most painful emotional experience?

_____

_____

_____

_____

_____

6) What steps do you still need to take to effectively deal with that experience?

_____

_____

_____

_____

_____

CHAPTER 6
Those Darn Rules

GROWING UP WE HAD RULES in our home like anyone else. Some of these rules were good rules, but today I would consider some of these rules quite silly. I shall refer to these rules as the "good rules" and the "silly rules." Some of these rules were given to mankind by God, but most of the rules we had were man-made.

First, a review of the rules given to us by God. These rules are commonly called The Ten Commandments. We all know the drill: honor God, honor parents, sex is something to be shared only with your spouse of the opposite gender, don't lie, don't murder and be content with your own stuff rather than envying your neighbor's stuff. God has a bunch of other rules but He tells us they can all be summed up by His Two Great Commandments. These are to love God with all your heart, soul, mind and strength and to love your neighbor as yourself.

God's rules were a big part of the rules in my home growing up and I would consider them to be among the "good rules." Today I believe that following these rules is essential if I am to have any chance for a great quality of life. They may be God's rules but they are for my own good. It's like God gave us the perfect recipe for a fruitful and happy life, but whenever we tamper with that recipe it never turns out quite the same or as good as it could be. If everyone lived by these rules our world would be a much better place.

Then there are the man-made rules. There have been many men throughout the ages who seemed to have thought that God didn't complete His job properly and felt that it was their duty to make more rules for us to live by. While some of these man-made rules are good others are nothing more than someone else trying to tell me how I'm supposed to live my life.

Before I start writing about the silliness of some of these man-made rules I want to be up front about my thoughts regarding rules. Since it is God's Universe He has the right to make whatever rules He likes. Since parents are responsible for their children they have the right to make whatever rules they think best for their home. Since the government is responsible for public health and safety they have the right to make whatever rules they deem best for society. While God is infallible, both parents and those in government are human and we humans have repeatedly demonstrated that we are perfectly capable of making rules that are not only silly, but are often unduly burdensome or even wrong.

Another obvious point that I'd like to mention is that governments don't make rules (laws), people do; laws and rules are made by people in positions of power. If those who have been elected are making silly or wrong rules then we have the responsibility to remove these people from their positions and elect others who display more sense. We have no cause to complain about our city, state or nation if we are not embracing our duty to vote and vote responsibly. That's enough of my political rantings.

So...back to the man-made silly rules; here are a few examples of some of these rules. They were part of my growing up and were strictly enforced in my childhood home. I can assure you that they were not carried forward into my home once I was married and had children of my own.

- We could not go to a theater to watch a movie.

- We could not go swimming in any pool or beach where there were members of the opposite sex present in the water.

- We could not play any games where "poker" (playing) cards or dice were used.

- We could not dance.

- We could not drink any alcoholic beverage or eat at any establishment that served alcohol.

- My sisters were not allowed to wear shorts or pants.

- Military style haircuts were required for the boys.

One may not fully grasp how these rules affect a kid while growing up so let me give just one example. When I was in Junior High School our PE classes would sometimes involve dancing. Our PE teachers would try to provide social and cultural enrichment through some form of folk dancing or square dancing to break up the monotony of those boring activities like dodge-ball or rugby. During these times where dancing was the designated PE activity, I was forbidden to participate and required to watch from the side-lines. I really didn't care much about not being able to dance but it was quite embarrassing having to explain things to every member of my class. When I would tell my friends that my parents wouldn't allow me to dance my friends would always ask why. I had no intelligently honest answer.

These rules were not unique to my home. When I went off to a Christian College I found that many of these same silly rules were waiting for me there as well and that many of my college friends also came from homes with similar silly rules.

When I was growing up my father was a minister. I believe that all of the silly rules listed above were honest attempts by my parents to keep me and my siblings out of trouble. In the "religious" world that they knew these rules were normal and I harbor no ill feelings toward my parents for having them. Today, I believe that most Christian Colleges and Christian homes have seen the silliness of these types of rules and no longer have or enforce them.

There were a few other rules that were part of my upbringing that others might find silly but that I believe were and still are good rules. These rules may have been intended to control my actions but living by these rules was a benefit to me because of the disciplines and behaviors I've developed as a result.

The first of these beneficial good rules was the strictly forbidden use of any tobacco product. I had absolutely no problem with that rule and today, some forty years after leaving my parents care, I have never had a chew or smoked anything including cigars, cigarettes or even what misguided folks call the "recreational" stuff. I discovered several years ago that I am badly allergic to smoke and I find it extremely difficult to even breathe when I'm around it.

Both of my sons-in-law occasionally enjoy a cigar; I even gave one son-in-law a couple of "Cubans" that had been given to me because I had no use for them and knew that he would enjoy them. I have no problem when a friend or a family member lights up a cigar once in a while, but please don't expect me to hang around while they enjoy it.

Not only is buying cigarettes expensive and habitual smoking bad for one's health, habitual smoking can cost the smoker a great deal more. As a real estate broker I would tell any smoker in my employ-ment that their habit cut their commission earning potential by at least twenty-five percent. When challenged on this claim I would explain to them that smokers have no idea how much they, their clothes and their car reek of smoke and that at least twenty-five percent of their potential clients will never use their services be-cause they can't stand the smell. It's like going to a very fine restau-rant and being waited on by a waiter with such bad body odor that you simply cannot enjoy the meal or the experience. Just as the waiter is clueless about his BO problem so are smokers clueless about their offensive reek. As a matter of fact "reek" is a Scottish word for "smoke."

There is additional cost for those who smoke in their home. Smokers don't typically notice the smoke odor in their homes but non-smokers will notice it immediately. Owners of homes that have a strong smoke odor are often unable to sell their home to anyone other than another smoker. But if they do sell to a non-smoker typically they must reduce their selling price by about fif-teen percent. Non-smoking home buyers will discount the price they are willing to pay by the number of dollars required to make the stench go away. I'm fairly confident that the same would apply to automobiles as well.

For a variety of reasons habitual smoking makes no sense and I am very grateful that my parents had the "no tobacco" rule in our home when I was growing up.

In addition to the "no tobacco" rule, my parents enforced a strict "no profanity" rule. If we were watching a television show when a four-letter word was mentioned the television was immediately turned off or at least the channel was changed. It was not uncommon to start watching a show only to have the channel changed two or three times before the television was finally just turned off.

If my parents heard me or a sibling using profanity, which by the way included words like piss, heck and darn; my mother would wash our mouth out with soap. She would do this by rubbing a bar of soap on our tongue or squirting dishwashing soap in our mouth. This only happened a few times but it indeed happened. I think of this unpleasant experience each time I see kids blowing bubbles at a birthday party and I'm fairly confident that I could guess where the idea for this popular child past-time originated.

I have not lived under my parent's roof for some forty years now but some of their rules still influence my life. As I mentioned earlier I have never smoked anything. Besides never smoking I have never consumed an alcoholic beverage, but I intend to have a glass of champagne on my 100th birthday. As an adult and no longer bound by my parent's rules I still adhere to a strict "no profanity" rule for my life. But even as strict as I might want to be about the use of profanity there have been a handful of times when my frustration or anger got the best of me and that filter between my brain and my mouth was caught in the off position.

The rules I have for myself are just that...for myself. I will not try to force them upon someone else because I know it would be of no use. Rules that I create for myself must come from my heart and my personal desire to improve who I am rather than someone else's idea as to how I should live. I have no problem with anyone who responsibly enjoys adult beverages and I'm not so extreme that I would turn off the television or walk out of a theater if occasional profanity is used. I'll walk out of a theater or turn off the television for other reasons, but not for occasional profanity; sometimes I think that I probably should.

I don't avoid the use of profanity for any moral or religious reasons; I just think that profanity should not be used in normal conversation because there are many people who find it offensive. How can anyone think that using the N word is irresponsible without having the same objection to the F word? I could never use either.

Additionally, the use of profanity sets a bad example to those who might be watching my life or looking to me for guidance and leadership. Most people would agree that those who use the N word are either uncouth or stupid; I believe my use of profanity would be the same. I would be telling people that I'm stupid, uncouth, have a very limited vocabulary or that I'm lacking in whit.

I am often surprised with the use of profanity by people that I respect and admire. I attended a real estate conference where an extremely well known motivational speaker was there to present the keynote address. There are only two things I remember about his speech:

1) He was drenched in sweat.
2) Every other word out of his mouth was of the four-letter variety.

I certainly can't fault him for the sweat but I would caution the manufacturer of his antiperspirant before using him as their spokesperson. However, this motivational speaker's use of profanity is quite another matter.

This speaker is wealthy and famous; you would know his name if I mentioned it. I had seen him on television and listened to his recordings on many occasions. Many will credit him for their financial success. I too had a great deal of respect for him and was thrilled when I had the opportunity to see him in person. He is a self-made man and I admire his tenacity to work through the hurdles that stood between him and his dream. He has much to be proud of.

While I'm quite certain that he doesn't give a ****, ****, **** about what I think or have to say, it's my book so I'll say it anyway. When he was speaking at this conference he was such a potty-mouth that I couldn't absorb anything he was attempting to communicate. Years of respect and admiration for the man were completely lost in just a few minutes. I cannot recall ever attending a similar event where I was more disappointed. A few years later he was speaking at another conference I attended and I didn't even bother going to listen to him.

For me it is not just a matter of profanity, it's a matter of being able to control my tongue because it's my tongue that seems to get me in more trouble than anything else. My tongue is the hardest thing for me to control. If I can find God's help in controlling my tongue I believe the rest of the things I need His help controlling will come much easier.

REFLECTION

1) What part of Perry's story did you identify with the most?

_____

_____

_____

_____

_____

2) What rules did you have growing up that you would consider silly today?

_____

_____

_____

_____

_____

3) Besides God's rules, what rules do you have for yourself that you believe make you a better person?

_____

_____

_____

_____

_____

4) Describe your views regarding the use of profanity?

_____

_____

_____

_____

_____

5) In what ways does your use of profanity change when you are at work or hanging out with other guys?

_____

_____

_____

_____

_____

6) In what ways is the man seen by your family different from the man seen by others?

_____

_____

_____

_____

_____

7) What are some of God's rules regarding controlling our tongue?

_____

_____

_____

_____

_____

CHAPTER 7

Encounters with Johnny Law

I PROBABLY SHOULD START THIS CHAPTER with a disclaimer. Yes, I know that most of the people in law-enforcement are good people just trying to do their job. I truly respect them and appreciate their willingness to put their lives on the line in service to their communities. But I must admit that some of my encounters with law-enforcement professionals have not left me with the warm and fuzzy feelings that should accompany my thoughts of those in uniform.

Without going into great detail I've had three encounters with law-enforcement officers where I think the officers did a remarkably professional job and handled themselves in a manner that was exemplary.

The first was when I was elk hunting. A herd of elk were running through the woods when I took a shot at one. The elk didn't act like it was hit so I waited for it to come into the next clearing and took what I thought was a second shot at the same elk. As it turned out they were not the same elk and I killed them both. I was not even aware that I had killed two elk until another individual who was not part of our hunting party discovered the second dead elk and felt that it was his duty to notify the authorities.

Once I learned of the error I acknowledged what had happened to the Game Wardens and took full responsibility. The Game Wardens were quite understanding; they gave me a small fine and only cited me for the minimum charge that they were allowed. They could have charged me with several other violations but told me that my cooperation had been rewarded. I'm fully aware that I could have said nothing and put the burden of proof on them but I knew that I was guilty and that the outcome could have indeed been much worse. I knew the truth and I just wanted the incident over and done with. That is exactly what happened. I paid the fine and my life immediately returned to normal. I believe that these men handled the situation professionally and were a credit to their uniforms.

Another encounter with the law was a time when I was caught speeding. I was living in Alaska at the time and flew down to Spokane, Washington on a business trip. I rented a car in Spokane and headed towards Lewiston, Idaho where I had some business meetings. As I drove into the town of Lewiston from the north, Highway 95 has a very steep three-mile stretch of road that winds its way down into the valley where this little community hides.

As I entered this steep stretch of road the speed limit suddenly dropped from 65 MPH to 50 MPH. I had taken my foot off of the accelerator to slow down but the road was so steep I wasn't slowing down very much at all. About a half mile later I saw an Idaho Highway Patrol car sitting just off the highway. Naturally, I applied my brakes to slow down.

Too late...I was busted...63 MPH in a 50 MPH speed zone. This Idaho State Patrol officer was kind and polite. Upon learning that I was in a rental car and from Alaska, he extended great mercy. After he lectured me about driving on steep roads (excuse me) offered me some helpful driving advice, he welcomed me to the area and then let me go. I could not believe he didn't give me a ticket.

My third encounter with law-enforcement personnel was when the FAA discovered that I had included some matches in a box I had shipped from Colorado to Alaska. This particular story is the subject of another chapter.

I also have three memorable encounters where Johnny Law's behavior was less than professional. The first was not a single event but rather a phase of harassment.

My family lived just outside of Hotchkiss, Colorado, a small farming community where the town itself was about six blocks wide and a mile long. During my High School years the most popular thing to do on Friday and Saturday nights was for three or four people to pile in one car and "cruise" Main Street. There were no traffic signals or stop signs so we would drive bumper-to-bumper from one end of town to the other at about 15 MPH, turning around in the hotel parking lot on one end of town and at a vacant lot on the other end. This exhaust sucking ritual would continue for three to four hours each Friday and Saturday night.

Main Street had two lanes going in each direction and we would regularly have conversations with carloads of Cruisers heading in the same direction but it was not uncommon to stop in the left lane and have a quick chat with a carload of Cruisers in their left lane heading in the opposite direction. I pitied any traveler who was actually heading somewhere whose journey took them through Hotchkiss on a Friday or Saturday evening.

When cruising Main Street, my '61 Apache-10 Chevy Pickup seemed to be the favorite target of the local cop; I was pulled over quite regularly. I don't recall any of my friends ever being pulled over. Barney

Fife was on a power trip and got his jollies by showing off his shiny, flashing red lights at my expense. Why this cop seemed to target me I will never know.

In all the times I was pulled over I never once received a ticket. I'm convinced that this small town policeman was simply bullying me because he had nothing better to do. I've since learned that small towns have small budgets and small towns are where those completing the Police Academy at the bottom of their class usually wind up. In other words, small towns don't usually employ the brightest bulbs in the chandelier.

Another incident involving law-enforcement that left a bitter taste in my mouth was the time I was traveling on Interstate 70 between Grand Junction and Fruita, Colorado. I traveled this stretch of interstate regularly and was on my way to an appointment. I knew well that the speed limit was 70 MPH which was the speed I was traveling. I was in the right lane when I came upon a line of six or seven cars also in the right lane but traveling only about 60 MPH.

I hit my left turn signal and passed the entire line of cars and noticed that the car leading the slower moving traffic was a Colorado State Patrol vehicle. After passing the State Patrol vehicle, never exceeding 70 MPH, I signaled and returned to the right lane. Immediately flashing lights came on and I pulled over.

I rolled down my window as the officer walked up to my car. "What's up," I asked.

"When you passed all those cars back there I didn't see you use your turn signal."

"I used my turn signal."

"I didn't say you **didn't** use your turn signal, I said I didn't **see** you use your signal."

"Well, how is it my fault if you're not paying attention?" (Note to self...avoid comments intended to make law enforcement officers look foolish!)

"Don't you get smart with me. I said I didn't see you use your signal so I want to check your signal to make certain they are working properly." The officer then walked to the back of my car and asked me to turn on my left signal, which I did and it worked fine.

He walked back to my window and I asked him, "Since you were in front of me why are you checking my rear signal? It would have been my **front** signal that you would have **not** seen!" I was making it clear that he knew that I knew that his actions were a load of BS.

"Oh Yeah," he said as he walked to the front of my car, requiring me to repeat the phony ritual for the front signal.

After checking the front signal he indicated that I was free to leave. I was only detained two or three minutes but it was a blatant abuse of his power to detain me because he didn't like the fact that I passed him rather than cowering behind him like all the other drivers had done. The officer's name was Fox and I almost filed a complaint against him but decided it would be a waste of time. Even though that incident was probably over twenty-five years ago it still gnaws at me every time I think about it. This man had been hired to protect and serve, not to abuse and bully.

Then there was another time when I was out rabbit hunting with my brother-in-law. We had been out for several hours and hadn't seen another soul all day when out of nowhere a Game Warden walked up to us and started visiting with us like we were old buddies. I hadn't killed anything so when the Game Warden asked what we were hunting I thought nothing about telling him that I was hunting rabbits. My brother-in-law didn't have a license so he wasn't actually hunting and we told him so.

We were in an area known as The Bookcliffs which is fairly desolate and has rolling terrain. There were no signs or road markings on the jeep trail that brought us into this unfamiliar area. I was perfectly legal, at least I thought. Apparently somewhere along the way we had crossed the border and were now in Utah, still thinking we were in Colorado. He asked to see my hunting license which I showed him. He then informed us that we were in Utah, not Colorado and I didn't have a Utah hunting license.

Before I knew what had happened he was walking away with my confiscated rifle in his hand as I stood there holding a very expensive piece of pink paper in my hand. I had no idea that I had done anything wrong, but I had incriminated myself with something I said without realizing it. To put it kindly, this Game Warden wasn't remotely close to what I would consider professional. However, after paying my fine, I eventually got my rifle back.

REFLECTION

1) What part of Perry's story did you identify with the most?

_____

_____

_____

_____

_____

2) What encounters have you had with the law where you felt the officer handled the situation professionally?

_____

_____

_____

_____

_____

3) Describe any unpleasant encounters you have had with law-enforcement officers.

_____

_____

_____

_____

_____

4) To what extent do you believe that we should follow man's laws?

_____

_____

_____

_____

_____

5) In what ways does following God's laws differ from following man's laws?_____

_____

_____

_____

_____

6) What injustices do you see that are being promoted by the laws of our nation? _____

_____

_____

_____

_____

7) Describe your personal duty and responsibility to change injustices within society? _____

_____

_____

_____

_____

8) What should be our response when we have strong moral or ethical objections to a law?_____

_____

_____

_____

_____

CHAPTER 8
More Encounters with Johnny Law

HAVE A FEW OTHER JOHNNY Law stories that have nothing to do with the professionalism of law-enforcement officers but are just somewhat amusing.

I have been driving for over forty years and have never had a speeding ticket. Please understand that when I say that I have never had a speeding ticket it is not because I feel I have some sort of badge of honor. No, I say this because I want you to feel the intense pressure that this abnormality places on me. I want you to feel the heavy weight that accompanies such a claim. In some sick sort of way I think I'd like to get a speeding ticket just so I can get it over and done with. It is exhausting going through life wondering when the hammer will finally fall.

I have actually planned my reaction to my first speeding ticket and I'm certain that the officer who gives it to me will never forget it. When I get that first ticket I'm going to make that officer think he just won the lottery by heaping on him as much praise and congratulations as I can possible muster. I want this officer to feel just like Pat Garrett did when he finally got Billy the Kid. When I'm done with this officer he will believe that he has accomplished something very special and has done a great service to me and to all of mankind.

When I say I have never received a ticket for speeding that in no way implies that I have not deserved more than my fair share of them…I've just never been caught. When I was a freshman in college I attended my sister's wedding in Casper Wyoming. The morning following her wedding, about 5am, I left Casper to return to college in Nampa, Idaho. Fifty-seven minutes after I left Casper I arrived in Shoshoni, Wyoming which is exactly one hundred miles away. One hundred miles in fifty-seven minutes is an average speed of 105 MPH. Not only was I driving way too fast, but I was driving while it was still dark on a two-lane highway through an area loaded with big game. One hundred and eighty miles beyond Shoshoni I stopped in Jackson, Wyoming to fill up with gas. While filling up I noticed that I had a tire so badly worn that I could see the cord under the tread so I bought a couple of new tires on the spot. That drive from Casper to Shoshoni is probably the stupidest thing I have ever done.

Another time I made a road trip from Idaho where I attended college to Indiana where my parents lived. I was somewhere in Iowa on a two-lane highway where the terrain was exhaustingly flat and fields of crops made up the entire landscape. This was back when the speed limit throughout the United States was 55 MPH.

Even though it was in the middle of the afternoon it was not uncommon to drive for several miles before meeting another vehicle. Finally, after hours of driving there was a change of scenery. I could see a pimple rising above the smooth landscape next to the highway several miles away. I was traveling about 75 or 80 MPH and feeling very safe in doing so. I kept my eye on this object that served to disrupt the horizon and as I got within a few miles of it I could tell that it was a very large grain silo.

A few minutes later I was now close enough to tell that the silo was about fifty or sixty feet tall and about thirty feet in diameter. It was standing about thirty yards off of the road. As I approached the silo I noticed that there was not just one huge grain silo but there were actually two silos. They were the same size and setting next to each other, in line, parallel to the road and about twenty feet apart so that from a distance the first silo hid the second one.

As I sped by these silos I looked over and guess what I saw sitting between them…an Iowa State Trooper vehicle. "Oh crap," I said. I lifted my turn signal and pulled off of the highway since there was no doubt I was guilty and may as well just get it over with. I sat in my car just off the road for three or four seconds taking a couple of deep breathes in anticipation of getting my first ticket. Now completely stopped and setting on the highway shoulder I looked into my side mirror expecting to see the Trooper's car pulling up behind me. There was no sign of the State Patrolman. I continued to wait on the side of the highway for another full minute; surely he was coming. He never came. I could not believe it. I pulled back onto the road and resumed my trip in humble gratitude while shaking my head in bewilderment.

All I can figure is that this State Patrol Officer must have been taking a nap or trying to become better acquainted with some local farm girl. Why he never came out from between those silos I will never know but I wasn't about to hang around any longer to try to figure it out. Another bullet dodged.

Another law-enforcement story that exposes a little more of my darker side also involves elk hunting. But to set the stage a bit it would be helpful to know that my family isn't big on buying our meat from a grocery store. While living in Colorado for thirty years we filled our freezer with the deer and elk we hunted. When we lived in Alaska for ten years it was halibut and salmon that filled the freezer. Now we live on a farm and raise chickens and beef but still have plenty of deer hanging around our place whenever we are inclined to hunt them.

Over my lifetime I have probably bagged around thirty-five elk and fifty deer. But if you were to look at me and do the math you would quickly figure out there is no way I could have legally done what I claim unless I was one of those Duck Dynasty types who live to hunt and travel all over the country in pursuit of the kill. No offense to the Duck Dynasty men, I like those guys and would love to meet them some day.

To feed our family it would take more than one deer and one elk each year. To have any chance of bagging multiple deer and elk each year it required that my wife get involved with the overall hunting strategy. Big-game hunting has provided some of my life's fondest memories, but hunting also accounts for some of my most *miserable* life experiences. Hunting may take place in the warmth and tranquility of an Indian summer day or our hunting season may come complete with a 40-MPH wind and snow storm. Unlike some hunters, my idea of fun is not spending a week huddled around a campfire trying to keep warm and dry under a makeshift plastic canopy while trying to avoid the smoke swirled around by a fickle wind.

I've taken my wife hunting on two occasions. There are two occasions because the first was one of those glorious times when everything worked as you would hope: warm weather, no rain, abundant game and quick kills. We showed up, it was nice and we went home before anything could spoil the occasion. Our second hunting trip was a bit different. Had the second hunt been our first hunt there would have never been a second hunt. We would have had two hunts in one…our first and our last. There's this saying, "If momma ain't happy…ain't nobody happy." And on that subject that's all I dare say.

Colorado big game hunting laws prohibit what is called "party hunting." What this means is that one hunter cannot shoot an animal to fill the license of another hunter. In other words if you have a license to shoot a cow elk only *you* can shoot your cow elk. It's a ridiculous law that is ignored about as much as the laws that prohibit people from talking on cell phones while driving, but don't get me started on that.

Since we needed more meat than I could provide on my own and our attempts at hunting according to the letter of the law hadn't worked out, we decided to get creative. No, let me rephrase that. We ignored the law. My wife and I would both get deer and elk licenses each year and I would fill them. My wife would stay at home and do her thing and I would show up with the meat.

On one such occasion I had been hunting with some friends for a few days. After hunting they dropped me off at my house late one evening and helped me hang a cow elk and a five-point bull elk in our garage to cure for a couple of days. When I say five-point bull elk I mean five points on each side which would be a ten-point bull elk using the EGO point-count method so commonly used in Texas and the mid-west states.

Someone saw us hanging these elk and felt compelled to report it to the Department of Fish and Game. About an hour after getting home and just as I was finishing up the work in the garage our doorbell rang. I opened the door to find two Game Wardens standing in front of me.

They told me that they had received a report of elk being brought in under cover of night and wanted to know what I had to say about the report. I had nothing to fear so I ushered them into the garage to see that all was in order. In Colorado your game "tag" is to remain attached to the animal at all times until it is processed and even then it must be available for inspection. But I had forgotten that I had taken the tags off of the animals to skin them. When they asked about the tags I told them that I had taken them off to skin the animals and had just finished up and hadn't reattached them yet. This was completely true.

I went into the house to get the tags out of my coat pocket and realized that my wife had not filled out or signed her tag. She was upstairs in bed suffering from a really bad head-cold. I quickly filled out her tag and then headed upstairs to our bedroom to have her sign it while the Game Wardens were still waiting for me in the garage.

My wife just had to know what was going on so I gave her as quick of an explanation as twelve seconds would permit. I told her to stay put and that I would take care of everything. Do you think that staying put is what she did? No way. I married a fine woman and I'm glad that she has a mind of her own, but not on this occasion. I was in the garage bragging about my wife's hunting skills to these Game Wardens. Just as I'm telling them how she killed her cow elk she appeared in the doorway to see for herself what was going on. When she showed up I knew I was toast. My wife wouldn't tell a lie to save her own neck, much less mine.

One of the Game Wardens turned to my wife and asked, "Ma'am, is it true that you have been hunting and you shot this elk?"

Oh how I love my wife. All she said was, "How do you think I got this cold? Now if you'll excuse me I'm going back to bed," as she turned and walked back into the house.

The Game Wardens looked at each other with a dumbfounded look of disappointment. I don't know if they believed the story but they indicated that everything looked to be in order. After they cautioned me to be more careful about keeping the tags attached to the carcasses, they started on their way. As they were leaving one of them turned to me and said, "That's a really nice bull you've got there, congratulations."

My final story about my encounters with the law also involves hunting. Deer season was coming to an end but I still had a doe tag to fill. Doe tags are usually quite easy to fill and I still had a couple of days so I wasn't in any big panic or rush to get out into the woods. I had taken the day off from work and my dad was coming by in the afternoon to ride along with me as I did a little "road hunting." "Road hunting" is what we call it when we drive around the nearby National Forest on primitive jeep trails looking for game from the comfort of our vehicle.

If we saw what we were hunting for we would certainly follow the letter of the law. We would stop, turn off our vehicle, step out of the vehicle, put on our florescent orange vest and florescent orange hat, take our rifle out of its case, step away from the vehicle, load our rifles, walk the required twenty yards distance from the road and take a nap. I may as well take a nap because by the time you do all that stuff any animal is now five miles away and I'm just not that great at five-mile shots. Just maybe there was a time or two when I might have forgotten all the legally required steps and just shot the animal while seated in my pickup. Right now something about silly rules comes to mind.

Before heading out to go road hunting with Dad on this particular afternoon I had spent the better part of the morning butchering chickens. Processing chickens can be very bloody work and I frequently used the tailgate of my pickup as an outdoor workbench for this messy chore. When a chicken's head is removed from its neck a chicken will naturally flop all over the place if it is not restrained. As part of the butchering process I would remove the chicken's head from its neck then toss the chicken into the back of my pickup where it would flop around until it became lifeless.

I had just finished the last chicken when Dad showed up. The back of my pickup was a very bloody mess and I didn't want to waste any valuable hunting time washing it out. I figured I'd probably shoot a deer and that it would get all bloody again so why not just wait until I was done with the deer and clean up both bloody messes at the same time. It was a splendid plan.

Dad and I drove around the mountains for a few hours and didn't see any deer. When it became too dark to hunt any longer we started making our way towards home. Just as we were coming off of the mountain road and about to reach the highway we encountered a "game check." For those unfamiliar with game checks, game checks are like DUI checkpoints. Game checks are where Game Wardens park their vehicle just around a sharp curve on a mountain road where they surprise unsuspecting hunters with illegal searches of their vehicles and inspections of their rifles.

As we pulled up to the game check the Game Warden stepped out into the road and motioned for me to stop. By now it was dark. The Game Warden walked up to my window with his flashlight shining in my face. He started asking the routine questions. The game check was no big deal; I was sure that I had been through this drill as many times as he had. I cut him off after his first question and skipped right to the bottom line assuring him that we hadn't seen or killed anything and were just heading home. It appeared to be a very short encounter and he seemed satisfied.

Just as I was pulling away the Game Warden pointed his flashlight into the back of my pickup and shouted for me to stop. "What's with all this blood?" he demanded. I tried to explain where the blood came from but he wasn't buying what I was selling. He was positive that I had killed something and dumped it as soon as I saw the game check. His questioning was relentless. He insisted that we stay put in the vehicle while he walked back up the road for a couple hundred yards looking for evidence in the brush with his flashlight. Reluctantly, he finally let us go. I'm sure that Game Warden, to this day, is still convinced of my guilt.

REFLECTION

1) What part of Perry's story did you identify with the most?

_____

_____

_____

_____

_____

2) Describe a situation where you were guilty of breaking the law, should have been caught yet got away without penalty?

_____

_____

_____

_____

3) Describe how you felt when that happened?

_____

_____

_____

_____

_____

4) Describe a situation where you were not guilty yet someone in authority thought you were?

_____

_____

_____

_____

_____

5) Describe how you felt when that happened? _____

_____

_____

_____

_____

6) Describe the details of any time you have spent in jail or prison? _____

_____

_____

_____

_____

7) What role should punishment and forgiveness play in our life and our justice system?

_____

_____

_____

_____

_____

8) Knowing our own guilt, what should be our attitude when it comes to forgiving others?

_____

_____

_____

_____

_____

CHAPTER 9

Blowing Up Airplanes

"ON SEPTEMBER 11, 2001, *19 militants associated with the Islamic extremist group al-Qaeda hijacked four airliners and carried out suicide attacks against targets in the United States. Two of the planes were flown into the towers of the World Trade Center in New York City, a third plane hit the Pentagon just outside Washington, D.C., and the fourth plane crashed in a field in Pennsylvania. Often referred to as 9/11, the attacks resulted in extensive death and destruction, triggering major U.S. initiatives to combat terrorism and defining the presidency of George W. Bush. Over 3,000 people were killed during the attacks in New York City and Washington, D.C., including more than 400 police officers and firefighters."*[1]

September 11, 2001 indeed was a tragic day for the United States. But I too have a story that came about as a result of 9/11 and I am so glad it never made any newscasts or headlines.

On 9/11 the Federal Government grounded all air traffic while trying to figure out what had happened. Over the next few days air traffic

---

1   http://www.history.com/topics/9-11-attacks

slowly was allowed to resume but anything to do with airplanes was super sensitive for the next few months. During this time I had just completed negotiations for the purchase of a business and was in the process of relocating my family from Colorado to the incredible State of Alaska.

Our middle child, Amy, was a senior in high school and my wife and I didn't feel it would be fair to move her before her graduation. I moved to Alaska in December of 2001 and lived in a furnished apartment until the rest of the family could join me after Amy's graduation in May of 2002. During this period, January through May, I returned to Colorado each month to spend a week with my family.

In exchange for uprooting my wife from all of her friends and moving her to a place where everyone lives in igloos and spends their days hunting whales in the dark, I made her some promises. I promised that when we moved into our new home in Alaska she could buy all new furniture and appliances. We sold or gave away nearly everything we owned so we could move to Alaska with all of our possessions packed into our Toyota Tacoma with a small U-Haul in tow. Consequently, we were very limited in terms of what we could take with us.

Each month when I returned to Colorado for a week I packed up four or five boxes of stuff that I needed to run my business, starting with the items that I most urgently needed. I took these boxes to the UPS store and had them shipped to my office in Alaska where they would usually be waiting for me upon my return.

When I was in Colorado with the family that March, I followed this same routine of packing a few boxes. Having already shipped the most essential items, I was now boxing up less important things. These included: old records, tax returns and a few business books that I hadn't cracked in years. After loading the last of these non-essential business items my final box was only half full. So rather than ship a half-empty box I just started grabbing things off the closet shelves and shoved them into the box; a couple of hats, a baseball glove, some workout clothes and just whatever would fit into the available space.

Once again I took these boxes to the UPS store where I was asked the usual questions about hazardous materials, flammable objects, illegal drugs, etc. etc., to which I confidently replied, "No Ma'am, it's just a bunch of books and papers." I finished out my week with the family and returned to Alaska hopeful that my final shipment would be waiting for me.

When I returned to Alaska my UPS shipment was not waiting for me. I thought very little about it because there wasn't anything in those boxes that I urgently needed. After a few days had passed and still no shipment I started to wonder and then finally, after about two weeks, I called UPS and see if they had any idea what had happened to my boxes. When I finally finished negotiating the telephone maze and was able to talk to a live person, all that he said was, "Uh, Mr. Underwood, uh yeah, uh you need to uh come down to our office." Of course my imagination was going all sorts of places as I hopped in my car and made the twenty-minute drive out near the airport where the UPS office was located.

When I arrived at the UPS office they were waiting for me. Within five seconds of walking in the door I was introduced to this stocky short fella who may not have had much height but obviously had a great deal of power, at least at this UPS office. This manager, complete with his Napoleon Syndrome, started explaining to me that one of his delivery guys was delivering my boxes when he dropped one. When my box hit the ground it broke open causing the contents to be exposed. Unapologetic about damaging my stuff, Mr.

Napoleon proceeded to rip into me for about five straight minutes about trying to blow up his airplane, I'm serious, he called it "my airplane." His lecture continued with outlandish accusations as to how my carelessness could have set fire to his terminal.

I was totally taken aback. I had no idea what Napoleon is ranting about and was wondering if his tirade had been directed towards the wrong person. I asked him to explain. He then picked up and showed me a ceramic jar. In the tone of a trial lawyer he said, "This is what I'm talking about."

Now it all made sense. In my haste to fill up the final box before shipment one of the things I grabbed was a ceramic jar about six inches tall and four inches in diameter. This jar looked like a little honey pot. Over the years I had collected matchbooks from various business establishments and stored them in this ceramic jar. The matches were just a novelty and really had very little value to me. But apparently matches are a hazardous material and according to Napoleon, "They have the potential of spontaneous combustion which might blow up one of my planes."

I graciously endured the remainder of his tongue-lashing, humbly apologized to Mr. Napoleon, loaded my boxes of hazardous materials into my car and headed back to my office relieved that this ordeal was finally over. NOT. I'm not sure what his reasoning or motives might have been, but for some unknown reason, whether from mandate or simply from spite, Mr. Napoleon was compelled to report this "incident" to the FAA.

I learned of the FAA's involvement when I returned to my office from my chat with Napoleon. I arrived at my office to find a phone message from an FAA investigator asking me to give him a call. It was about 3pm on a Friday afternoon when I found the investigator's message and I immediately returned his call.

So to reset the stage, I had just come from a tongue-lashing where I was accused of trying to blow up an airplane and set a shipping terminal on fire; every law-enforcement agency in the entire USA was extremely sensitive with any matter dealing with airline sabotage due to the events of 9/11; and it was 3pm on a Friday afternoon and I had an FAA investigator looking for me. I don't know about your experiences, but for me I've never had much luck catching any federal employee in the office on a Friday afternoon and today would be no different.

I stayed in my office until about 6pm hoping for a return call from the investigator. I finally gave up and went to my apartment. I am normally not the nervous type, but panic began to settle in. I became a nervous wreck. I was totally consumed by the fear of my life crashing into a thousand little pieces. I tell you the truth when say that I did not get a single minute of sleep for the next two days and three nights.

I figured this would definitely involve jail-time, expensive defense attorneys costing hundreds of thousands of dollars, newspaper headlines, confiscation of everything I owned, divorce, being disowned by every friend and family member and on and on it went. The next three days were the longest of my life and I knew there was no one I could talk to that could say anything to change what I was dealing with.

Monday morning *finally* arrived. Soon after returning to work I heard back from the investigator. We made an appointment for him to come to my office. Prior to this time my experiences with law-enforcement officers, with a few exceptions, had not been what I would call...pleasant. My history with law enforcement people has not been a good one. Often I have found them to be bullies and abusers of their power and position, but that's a different chapter.

I had every expectation that he would come to my office at the appointed time, slap the cuffs on me and haul me off to wherever it is they haul hardened criminals.

The investigator showed up at the appointed time and to my surprise he was a down-to-earth reasonable sort of guy. I had two guest chairs in my office, facing my desk. Whenever I had just one guest it was always my custom to get up from my desk and go around to the other side and sit in one of the guest chairs next to my guest. When the investigator came in I offered him a chair and sat in the guest chair next to him. He leaned back in his chair, made himself comfortable and asked me to tell him what happened. I then told him my story.

After telling my story the investigator said, "I believe you. You may have screwed up but you are no criminal. I opened all of your boxes and saw what was in them before you picked them up. It was a strange combination of stuff, but nothing to cause concern. Unfortunately I can't just let you walk because I have to throw a bone to the folks who turned this in."

It turned out that if I agreed to pay for and attend an all-day class on hazardous shipping the investigator would call it good. So I paid the $100 tuition and wasted an entire day sitting through a class where I would learn absolutely nothing of value to me. And I was extremely happy to do so. The hazardous shipping course instructor had been given a heads-up on who I was and why I was there. At the end of the day, just prior to administering the exam, the instructor, as if to validate the importance of his course, told the entire class why I was there before excusing me. Unlike the rest of the class I had no need for the certification this class provided and therefore didn't have to take the exam. I know his intent was to humiliate me. But from the looks in the eyes of the other thirty people attending I could tell that by not having to take the exam I held the more enviable position.

A few weeks after taking the hazardous shipping course I received a letter from the FAA stating that they had completed their investigation and found no intent of illegal or criminal activity and that the case had been closed. The case may have been closed but the FAA was not quite done with me.

My business required that I travel outside of Alaska four or five times each year. After my UPS/FAA incident I quickly noticed that **every** time I flew anywhere I was "randomly" selected for a more thorough search, including a body search and a physical search of any carry-on items. The "random" searches had been going on for a couple of years when I had the most impressive of all.

I had just attended a conference in Chicago which ended about five hours before my departure flight time. This gave me about three hours to kill before I needed to be at O'Hare International Airport. For me three hours was not enough time too to confidently enjoy taking in another site of the city so I decided to go to the airport and hangout there until it was time to leave. For exercise I walk about five miles each day so after arriving at the airport and going through security I just briskly walked around the terminal for about an hour and a half.

After my walk, and still two hours before my flight would board, I bought a sandwich and headed to my gate to relax, eat and read until it was time to go. I was in the seating area at my gate, minding my own business. There wasn't another soul anywhere in sight. I kid you not; there was no other person seated at my gate or the gate next to me or the two gates opposite. This area of the terminal was so empty that I could have died from a heart attack and no one would have noticed my cold body for at least an hour.

It had been at least two hours since I had gone through security where I had my last interaction with another human being except to pay the cashier when I bought my lunch. I was as alone as is possible in an international airport when two uniformed officers, a man and woman, walked up to me. The male officer addressed me, "Mr. Underwood, we are with TSA and you have been randomly selected for an additional search of your person and your carry-on items." These officers did not walk up to me and *ask* my name... they walked right up to me and *stated* my name.

I gave them my best, "you've got to be kidding me" look. I then looked at the empty terminal to my left, then to the empty terminal to my right and said, "Random huh?" He gave me his best, "don't be a jerk, I'm just doing my job" smile and replied, "Yes Sir."

After about four years of being searched every time I traveled, without exception, I remember going through airport security and actually being surprised that I wasn't "randomly" selected for search. Even though my case had been closed I'm confident that my episode had landed me on some FAA watch list. The searches had finally ended.

REFLECTION

1) What part of Perry's story did you identify with the most?

_____

_____

_____

_____

_____

2) Describe a situation where you experienced intense fear?

_____

_____

_____

_____

_____

3) In what ways can fear cause us to make poor choices?

_____

_____

_____

_____

_____

4) Describe the consequences of one poor choice you have made. _____

_____

_____

_____

_____

5) How do you think others would describe your reputation?

_____

_____

_____

_____

_____

6) How would you describe your reputation?

_____

_____

_____

_____

_____

7) In what ways is your reputation important?

_____

_____

_____

_____

_____

8) If you had the power to go back and change one thing you have done that impacted your reputation (or could impact your reputation if it became known), what would it be?

_____

_____

_____

_____

_____

CHAPTER 10

The Shortcut

IN THE COMPETITIVE WORLD OF sports the fame and fortune of professional athletes depends on their ability to perform. One poor performance might be forgiven but that's about it. Fans are fickle and past performances, regardless of how spectacular are quickly forgotten. The pressure to keep your edge or gain some competitive advantage is intense and keeping that edge or gaining a competitive advantage, done legally is very hard work. There is always the temptation to take the "shortcut."

In the 1919 World Series of Baseball the Chicago White Sox were defeated by the Cincinnati Reds. So what's the big deal about a World Series a hundred years ago? In this World Series eight White Sox players were later accused of intentionally losing games in exchange for money from gamblers. The players were acquitted in court but were nevertheless banned for life from baseball and the 1919 World Series has come to be known as the Black Sox Scandal.

Someone would need to be an ardent fan of baseball to name more than a handful of players from that era, but the eight players banned from baseball for their involvement in the Black Sox Scandal are among the most notorious. I think that all men want to leave a legacy, but the legacy of these men is one that no man wants. Here is what Wikipedia has to say about these eight players from the White Sox baseball team who were banned from baseball by Commissioner Kenesaw Landis for their involvement in the fix.

- **Eddie Cicotte**, pitcher, died on May 5, 1969, had the longest life; living to the age of 84. Admitted involvement in the fix.

- **Oscar "Happy" Felsch**, center fielder, died on August 17, 1964, at 72.

- **Arnold "Chick" Gandil**, first baseman. The leader of the players who were in on the fix. He did not play in the majors in 1920, playing semi-pro ball instead. In a 1956 *Sports Illustrated* article, he expressed remorse for the scheme, but claimed that the players had actually abandoned it when it became apparent they were going to be watched closely. According to Gandil, the players' numerous errors were a result of fear that they were being watched. He died on December 13, 1970, at 82.

- **"Shoeless" Joe Jackson**, the star outfielder, one of the best hitters in the game, confessed in sworn grand jury testimony to having accepted $5,000 cash from the gamblers. He later recanted his confession and protested his innocence to no effect until his death on December 5, 1951, at 64; he was the first of the eight banned White Sox players to die. Years later, the other players all said that Jackson had never been involved in any of the meetings with the gamblers, and other evidence has since surfaced that casts doubt on his role.

- **Fred McMullin**, utility infielder. McMullin would not have been included in the fix had he not overheard the other players' conversations. He threatened to tell all if not included. His role as team scout may have had more impact on the fix, since he saw minimal playing time in the series. He had the shortest lifespan, dying on November 20, 1952 at 61.

- **Charles "Swede" Risberg**, shortstop. Risberg was Gandil's assistant and the 'muscle' of the playing group. He went 2-for-25 at the plate in the World Series. The last living player among the Black Sox, he lived on until October 13, 1975, his 81st birthday.

- **George "Buck" Weaver**, third baseman. Weaver attended the initial meetings, and while he did not go in on the fix, he knew about it. Landis banished him on this basis, stating "Men associating with crooks and gamblers could expect no leniency." On January 13, 1922, Weaver unsuccessfully applied for reinstatement. Like Jackson, Weaver continued to profess his innocence to successive baseball commissioners to no effect. He died on January 31, 1956, at 65.

- **Claude "Lefty" Williams**, pitcher. Went 0–3 with a 6.63 ERA for the series. Only one other pitcher in baseball history has ever lost three games in one World Series, although it should be noted that the third game Williams lost was Game Eight – baseball's decision to revert to a best of seven Series in 1922 significantly reduced the opportunity for a pitcher to obtain three decisions in a Series. Williams died on November 4, 1959, at 66.

All of the great and wonderful things that these men may have done are forgotten yet they will forever be remembered for their involvement in this one act of cheating. I certainly would not want people (like me) writing about my indiscretions long after I'm dead. But most of these men lived another forty or so years beyond the 1919 Series and had to deal with this situation every day for their entire lives.

Taking the shortcut always means breaking the rules. If a professional athlete takes the shortcut and is caught everything changes or is lost. Endorsements are canceled, championships are forfeited, personal accomplishments are removed from the record books, some are kicked out of their sport and for those who remain a black cloud hangs over their career for as long as they continue to compete.

Even considering all of the money, fame and accomplishments I believe that the greatest thing lost for those caught cheating is trust and respect. And the greatest thing that a man can lose is the trust and respect that others have in him. If we don't have trust and respect we have nothing. This is true regardless of how rich or famous we might be.

I think men cheat because we know it is very unlikely that we'll get caught. I have no way to back it up, but I would guess that for every case where someone is caught lying, cheating or breaking the rules there are at least 1000 other cases where a guilty party is never caught. The world would be a much different place if we all walked around with a lie-detector hanging around our necks.

Can you imagine such a device? Each time the wearer told a lie it would flash or beep. I would love to be a businessman who had access to such a lie-detector device without any one knowing what it was. I would require every salesperson, lawyer or job applicant to hang the lie-detector around their neck before starting our meeting. Better yet, require it for every public appearance for anyone running for an elected position. Someday someone will invent such a device. I digress.

Lying and cheating are much the same. Once we've done it and don't get caught it becomes easier to do it the next time, one lie begets another. We all probably know someone who was unfortunate enough to get away with several lies when they were very young and has now become a habitual liar. They have lied to you so often there is nothing they say that you can trust. Every time they speak you think to yourself, "You're so full of it your eyes are brown." You know who I'm talking about. These people have one sure way of letting you know when they are lying…their lips move!

Even the really smart guys who know their way around the system sometimes get caught. Lance Armstrong comes to mind. Armstrong was a professional road racing cyclist who won the Tour de France seven consecutive times from 1999 to 2005. I'm not a huge fan of cycling but I had great respect for this American icon who gave his European counterparts a drubbing year after year.

I had never before had any interest in the Tour de France, but sometime during Armstrong's incredible run I took an interest in this one annual event. For years Armstrong's competitors accused him of doping but I never believed it for even a moment. In the end I lost all respect for Armstrong when he was stripped of those victories in 2012 after a protracted doping scandal and I never again had the least bit of interest in the Tour.

I too have cheated, lied and taken shortcuts. I would guess that any man who claims to never have done so is lying to me. But are my actions any different from Lance Armstrong's or the baseball players in 1919? Maybe. Maybe not. In the eyes of other men I believe that my actions would probably seem different, but in the eyes of God I think not.

Without igniting a huge debate about what constitutes a big sin, a little sin or even if there is a difference I will go on record by suggesting that there is a difference. "Yes officer, I ran the stop sign so give me my ticket and let me get on to that appointment that I'm now even later for," is one thing. Quite different is, "Yes officer, that is my wife's blood all over my hands but I really have no idea how that knife got stuck in her chest." The difficulty in determining the difference between the minor infractions and the major ones is knowing where to draw the line between the two. But no matter where we draw the line we instinctively know when we've done wrong and we instinctively know when what we've done is really bad.

I've recently noticed a pattern when men do something that they know is really bad or really wrong. It began with the first man, Adam, and continues today. This pattern happens in almost every situation where a man gets busted for some major sin, crime or infraction.

The first thing we all do is to **hide** what has been done. If we can hide it well enough, no one will ever know and we can go through life without anyone ever knowing the truth about us. It could be stealing from our employer, watching pornography, drinking too much, involvement in an abortion, using illegal drugs, having an affair or a million other things. Once the deed has been done we will do whatever we must and hide it at any cost. For most of our misdeeds this is where the process ends, at least we *think* it ends, because we have gotten very good at the hiding part. But every so often we get busted, our hiding doesn't work as planned and it's time to move to phase two.

Once something is no longer hidden and an accusation has been made the next thing we will do is **deny** it. In most cases someone will simply ask us a question about a situation and to deny the misdeed seems like an option we ought to at least try. If we deny the accusation we know that there is a good chance that the situation will be ended right then and there and we can go back into hiding mode.

This compulsion to deny remains even in those times where the accusation is accompanied with strong evidence against us. If a woman arrives home early from work to find her naked husband in bed with her naked best friend, denial would be pointless. In those cases where the evidence is overwhelming and denial would only make matters worse we will skip the denial phase and jump to the next phase, **blame**.

No man wants to admit to himself much less to anyone else that he is capable of doing something dreadfully evil or just really bad. If we can paint a picture that we are innocent victims and that our behavior was caused by the uncontrollable influence of some other evil or awful person, it might just get us off the hook. And if we can't find some evil person to blame, as Adam did with Eve, we can always resort to, "The Devil made me do it."

After our crime can no longer be hidden, the evidence to too compelling to deny and no one is buying our attempts to blame someone else we find ourselves facing our last option, somehow we find a way to **justify** our actions. To justify is similar to blame yet very different. When we justify we are saying, "Yes, I did this terrible thing and it was an act of my own doing. But what I did is what every other human being would have done if they were dealing with the same set of circumstances that I was dealing with at the time."

After all else has failed, many will be remorseful and apologize for their behavior. We can never truly know what is in another man's heart but most of the time when I hear some professional athlete say that he is sorry for his behavior what I think he is saying is not that he is *sorry for what he did* but that he is *sorry for having been caught.*

From the 1919 Chicago White Sox to Lance Armstrong to me, we all go through the hide, deny, blame and justify process. But when we're guilty we're guilty and no matter how successful we might be in our attempts to keep or sins secret there is only one way to truly remove our guilt and shame. We can never undo what has been done but if we truly are sorry for our misdeeds we will have a much better outcome if we express how sorry we truly are and ask for forgiveness. Sometimes this confession and asking for forgiveness needs to be with the people we've injured, sometimes it needs to be with God alone and sometimes it needs to be with both.

REFLECTION

1) What part of Perry's story did you identify with the most?

_____

_____

_____

_____

_____

2) List the people that come to mind who were once great in their profession but experienced great moral failure?

_____

_____

_____

_____

_____

3) In what ways have you applied the hide – deny – blame – justify process to your own misdeeds? _____

_____

_____

_____

_____

4) Prepare a mental list of your misdeeds that you are confident will never be discovered. _____

_____

_____

_____

_____

5) Describe what you think would be the absolutely worst thing that could happen if some of your past misdeeds were uncovered?_____

_____

_____

_____

_____

6) To what extent do you need to express sorrow and ask forgiveness for things you have done?

_____

_____

_____

_____

_____

7) Who do you trust that you can share these answers with and will hold you accountable to take whatever action is needed?

_____

_____

_____

_____

_____

CHAPTER 11

Wanna Play Some Poker?

HAVE CONVINCED MYSELF THAT I am a pretty good poker player. I love playing the game even when nothing is at stake. But it is even more gratifying when I end an evening with a little extra cash in my pocket. Poker has a variety of different games and dozens of variations of these games. My favorite game is "Omaha," but most of my poker playing has been in "Texas Holdem" tournaments. If you are not familiar with poker, no problem, because the different types of poker games is not the point of this story.

While I fancy myself to be a fairly good poker player I'm not crazy enough to think I can make a living at it. Most of the tournaments I've played in have had no entry fee or an entry fee of less than fifty dollars. I have won or placed in the top five in dozens of these little 50-100 player tournaments. But to keep things in perspective, the most expensive poker tournament entry fee I have ever paid was $300 and that was only after intensely agonizing over the high probability that my $300 would be gone and that I would be out of the tournament within a few hours. My fears were realized. Making the top forty in this 300+ player tournament just added to my pain;

I would have been "in the money" if only I could have survived one more hour.

When we lived in Eagle River, Alaska I would drive to Wasilla almost every Monday evening for about two years to play in a free "Texas Holdem" tournament. Gambling is illegal in Alaska so my poker habit was relatively cheap. My wife wasn't thrilled with my weekly poker game but to her credit she gave me very little pushback.

One summer my sister Crystal and her husband Bob came to Alaska to visit us. While they were there we did what every good Alaskan host does and showed them the wonders of the State. We went fishing for halibut and salmon, saw whales and sea lions on a wild-life cruise, toured the glaciers and ate awesome meals in quaint little restaurants in the coastal towns of Seward and Homer. Bob and I even went on a private flight in a small plane around the top of Denali, (AKA Mt. McKinley). For non-Alaskan folks who may have missed it the name was changed from Mt McKinley back to Denali in August of 2015, but Alaskans have always called it Denali. In one of the native languages Denali means "The Great One."

One afternoon while Crystal and Bob were visiting us I asked Bob if he had any interest in playing in a poker tournament. Since it was a free tournament I even offered to spring for his entry fee. Bob acknowledged that he knew nothing about poker, but since he was the adventurous type and would try anything once. "Count me in," he said.

I found a deck of cards, printed off a list of possible poker hands and gave Bob a thirty minute crash course on the rules of the game. While making the 45-minute drive to Wasilla I gave Bob a very simple strategy:

1) Fold every non-premium hand and avoid the big betting battles.
2) Don't try to figure out who is bluffing.
3) Avoid making any raises.
4) Keep your game simple
5) Just play your hand.

I was sure Bob would be knocked out of the tournament in the first hour because with poker, like so many other things, experience is the best teacher. Since Bob would surely be knocked out of the tournament early I was concerned about what he would do with himself for several hours if I were fortunate enough to remain in the game. My concern didn't stop us and off we went.

We arrived early at the hotel where the tournament was being held and I gave Bob a few more last-minute pointers and reviewed his strategy. I knew that I had dumped so much information on Bob that there was no way he could remember it all; it was like trying to give him a drink from a firehose. My hope was that the simplicity of the strategy would keep him from embarrassing himself and keep him in the game for a while.

There were about 120 players in this tournament and seating was done by random draw of the seating cards. It just so happened that Bob and I drew the same table so we started the tournament sitting across from each other. This enabled me to keep an eye on his play, giving him an encouraging nod or a subtle facial reprimand after he played each hand. About twenty minutes into the tournament a player at another table was knocked out and I was moved to take the newly vacated seat. Bob was now on his own.

As with most poker tournaments, this poker tournament had ten-minute breaks every hour and Bob managed to survive the first hour.

We found each other during the first break and we took this time to quickly review some of his play and I offered him whatever thoughts I could to help keep him alive. After the break the field of players started to thin and I would glance across the room to see if Bob was still playing. Each time I did I was glad to see he was still there.

With 120 players I knew that this tournament would go about 5 hours so we still had a long way to go *if* we were fortunate enough to remain in the game. The second break rolled around. The playing field had been cut from twelve tables to eight but Bob and I were both still in it. The weakest players had been eliminated and now the playing field would get much tougher. I thought that Bob had done extremely well to hang in the tournament for the first two hours but I knew there was no way he would survive the next one.

We kept on playing. I kept on glancing over. Bob kept on being there. Amazingly, he survived the next hour. The third hour is the most grueling hour in a tournament this size because this is where a lot of low-chip-stack players make "all-in" moves in their desperate attempt to survive and rebuild their pile of playing chips. A player may move all-in on a flush draw and any player holding a made straight is compelled to call. If the player hits his flush he doubles his chips but if he misses the draw he could be out of the tournament. This particular move and many other like it are high risk moves but with huge rewards if they work.

The break for the third hour came and we did more celebrating than strategizing. We headed into the fourth hour and we both made it through that one as well. We both started play in the fifth hour and not long afterwards the tournament was down to the final ten players where we all assembled at what is called the "final table."

At the final table my role as Bob's cheerleader changed. I wanted desperately for Bob to do well and that he had. I never in my wildest dreams would have thought he would make the final table. But once again Bob and I were playing at the same table, the final table, and if he were to outlast me in his very first poker tournament I would never hear the end of it…really.

When it was all done the tournament could not have ended more perfectly. To both of our amazement Bob finished in third place and I won first. He was able to bask in his incredible success and I didn't have to bear the brunt of his success.

Of all the awesome things we saw and did during Bob and Crystal's visit that poker tournament was the highlight for Bob. Even now, years later, when we reflect back on that trip they made to Alaska Bob will talk about that tournament more than anything else. He has every reason to be proud for what he accomplished that night.

I love to play poker and I can confidently say that I am not addicted to poker or to gambling. But to be honest, I know there have been times when I've come very close to becoming a slave to it. I have seen and played with many people who *are* addicted and I can see how easily a game like poker or some silly video game can take control of men.

I think every person has a propensity to be addicted to something. For me it's gambling. For some men it is pornography. For others it's drugs, alcohol or sex. For some it could be one or more of a host of other seemingly harmless interests like money, fame, food, work, sports or television.

Short of having all your friends and family hold some sort of in-tervention, how do you know when you're addicted or have an unhealthy obsession with something? Maybe you're not addicted right now, but what is it that you could easily become addicted to? I'm not exempt and neither are you or anyone else.

I'm no counselor, psychologist or therapist, but I don't think it's all that tough to figure out what we are addicted to or what we have a propensity to be addicted to. I think it's a matter of honestly answering a few simple questions:

- **Where do I spend my money?**

- **Where do I spend my time?**

- **What consumes my thoughts?**

- **If I wanted to leave a good impression on someone, what one behavior or habit would I most likely conceal?**

So how do I overcome an addiction? Or what can I do to keep from becoming addicted to whatever I could easily become a slave to (my addiction propensity)? Well, you start by doing what you've just done…you admit it to yourself…you identify the enemy…you call it what it is.

REFLECTION

1) What part of Perry's story did you identify with the most?

_____

_____

_____

_____

2) What advice would you offer a friend who has a gambling addiction? _____

_____

_____

_____

_____

3) Being completely honest with yourself, what harmful activity or activities are you addicted to or prone to be addicted to?

_____

_____

_____

_____

_____

4) If you have an addiction or became addicted to the thing you have a propensity to become addicted to, in what ways could this addiction be harmful to you or those you love?

_____

_____

_____

_____

_____

5) Not including a spouse, who do you know that you trust and could hold you accountable in overcoming your addiction or keep you from becoming addicted?

_____

_____

_____

_____

_____

6) What role do you see God playing in overcoming your addiction?

_____

_____

_____

_____

_____

7) If you have been addicted to something and have genuinely recovered or have learned to manage your addiction, what would you say to a friend who is struggling with the same thing?

_____

_____

_____

_____

_____

CHAPTER 12
A Deep Dark Family Secret

MY WIFE IS NAMED SUSAN. I affectionately call her Suzy, Sooz or Your Highness, but for everyday conversation she is simply Sue. When Sue was an infant she was given up by her mother and placed in a Foster Home. At the age of two Sue was adopted by her Great Aunt and Uncle who were the much younger sister and brother-in-law of her biological Grandfather. In other words as Sue was growing up she had an older cousin who was near the age of her adoptive parents that was actually her biological father.

Sue has always considered her adoptive parents as "her parents" or "mom and dad," but this story is more about her biological mother and the events that led to her adoption. Any future reference in this chapter to Sue's mother or father is referring to her biological parents rather than her adoptive mom and dad.

It is important to mention that Sue was adopted by a wonderful man and woman who loved her dearly. This couple had three other living children but the nearest in age to Sue was thirteen years old at the time Sue was adopted. Even as their son-in-law I had an amazing relationship with both of them and they always treated me as if I was one of their own kids. This story is not meant to be critical of how they handled Sue's adoption; their handling of the adoption was exactly as they had been instructed.

Even though my wife's adoption was performed within the family and she was informed about her adoption at a very early age, her adoption was never talked about. Any questions she would raise about her adoption were quickly brushed off. Sue could sense that there was something about her adoption that was being kept from her in an effort to protect her, but from what she did not know. It was like she was part of a deep dark family secret that everyone in the family knew about except her.

I know this to be true because when I came into the family picture any questions that I would raise were met with similar evasiveness. The attorney that handled Sue's adoption was another close family member and he had convinced the entire family that all Sue needed to know was that she was adopted and that her adoptive family had come to her rescue. No other details were ever to be shared. For fifteen years we tried to get information from the family about her adoption but mostly to no avail.

My wife's deep dark family secret turns out to be quite a fascinating story.

Over the years we had been able to gather a few isolated details of the story, but I had never felt compelled to get very involved because there just wasn't much information to go on. When my wife was in her mid-thirties she became more and more interested in the details of her birth family. I wouldn't call it an obsession but it was getting close to that. Totally out of the blue she would randomly ask me impossible questions about her birth mother fully expecting me to provide the answer. This was happening so frequently that it was starting to become a serious issue between us. I even suggested that she travel to visit the hospital on her birth certificate to get whatever information that they would provide.

Over the next few years my wife's interest in her past became more and more acute as questions about her family's medical history were becoming very relevant to her. It seemed that each time Sue had a doctor's appointment she was further encouraged to find out about her family history.

One day I insisted that my wife sit down with me and go over every bit of information we had and I would see what I could piece together. I wish I could say that my desire to help was out of a servant's heart and that my only concern was the welfare of my wife. But the truth is that I was tired of the endless discussion that never seemed to produce any meaningful outcome. In other words, I'm embarrassed to admit that I was just doing whatever I had to do to get her to shut up about it, it really was that bad.

When I started piecing things together here are the facts I had to work with regarding my wife's adoption:

- Sue's birth certificate indicated that she was born at a hospital in Medical Lake, Washington, a small town on the east side of the state near Spokane.

- Sue was adopted by her Great Aunt and Uncle on her biological father's side at the age of two.

- We knew the name of her biological father; he was a member of the family (her father was now her cousin). Sue was never allowed to meet her father even though he had made attempts to do so.

- We had very little information about Sue's mother or her mother's family but we had cause to believe that her mother had some sort of serious medical condition. We also had cause to believe that her medical condition caused her to be a ward of the state and that she might have lived in some sort of medical treatment facility. We did not know if she was still alive or dead.

- Sue had two older biological sisters, one adopted by other family members and another adopted outside the family and we knew the names of both sisters.

- During my wife's formative years the sister that had been adopted within the family had been spoken of as a cousin and my wife didn't learn about their true relationship until she was well into her teenage years. We were aware that this sister had had a very "troubled" life and trying to re-establish a relationship would be extremely difficult if not impossible.

- The sister adopted outside of the family had been given enough information to locate Sue. This sister had contacted Sue years earlier and we had her contact information but it was several years old. They had never met.

There was one more thing that proved to be the most helpful of all. At some point after my wife and I were married her parents gave her a newspaper clipping that they had held for over thirty years. This newspaper clipping was the printed article that provided the general public with the details of her biological parent's wedding. Articles such as this were common in the 1950's with small-town papers in need of anything newsworthy. How they obtained this newspaper article or why they held onto it was unknown. The date on the newspaper article indicates that it was printed several years before my wife had been born, much less adopted by her new family.

My wife had kept this article for about fifteen years without giving any thought as to how valuable it would be in helping her connect with her past. Included in this article were places, dates and names of the wedding party and their families. From this article we learned her mother's maiden name and the name of some of her family members. But most importantly this article provided the name of her mother's brother who stood in as Best Man. We now had the name of my wife's biological uncle.

At this time the internet was still relatively new but was developed enough for me to find three names that matched the name of this uncle. Only one match had a California address and this address was very close to the town where the wedding took place. I wrote down the name and phone number of the man matching the name in the article so my wife could place a phone call and put an end to the years of the uncertainty about her past. She refused to place the call.

Sue thought it would be best if I placed the call on her behalf. She also thought that it would be better if she was not in the room, she did not want to hear the conversation. I can't say that I under-stood her rationale but I've learned that my job is not to question her logic, just do as I'm told.

One ringy-dingy. Two ringy-dingy.

"Hello"

"Hello. My name is Perry Underwood and at first this call may seem to be a bit strange but in a few moments it will make a lot more sense. I'm calling on behalf of my wife and I believe that you might be her uncle. I'm going to read to you from an article about a wed-ding that took place about fifty years ago."

I read to him the first paragraph of the article which gave the date of the wedding and named the wedding party which included his name, Peter Wygle. I stopped after reading his name. "Are you the Peter Wygle mentioned in this article?"

"Yes I am!"

I went on to explain that my wife was the daughter of his sister, Sally and that I had a few questions I'd like to ask to get a better understanding of my wife's family history. I was very slow and deliberate in my conversation because it was obvious that I was speaking to an elderly man. I began asking questions about Sue's mother and he was happy to provide whatever information he could.

From our conversation I learned that Sue's mother, Sally had been admitted to a State Institution for the Mentally Disabled when she was in her late twenties and had passed away over thirty years earlier when she was in her late thirties, he wasn't sure just exactly when. I learned that Sue's mother had epilepsy and that her father had abandoned his family. Because of recurring seizures and an absent father, Sue's mother was unable to care for herself or their two girls. She became a ward of the state and was institutionalized. The two girls were placed in Foster Care and eventually adopted.

Uncle Peter was unaware that Sally had a third daughter, my wife. Sue was born in the State Institution during the time her mother was a patient. We have deduced that Sue most likely was the result of a conjugal visit by the absent father who had this habit of just showing up from time-to-time.

I had the information I was looking for so I thanked Uncle Peter for his time and hung up the phone. He didn't ask me to repeat my name at any point in the discussion and we did not exchange contact information or make any sort of indication that there would be further communication. I'm a "bottom line" sort of person; I had all that I needed and I thought we were done.

I gave Sue my report. It went something like this.

"Your mother had epilepsy and was in a state institution for the mentally disabled, the hospital where you were born in Medical Lake, Washington. She passed away back in the sixties when she was in her late thirties." End of story; we're done with that; it's time to move on.

I thought I had done a terrific job of piecing this whole thing together; I had solved the case and it was now closed. Boy was I wrong…AGAIN. You see I'm a "bottom line" sort of person but Sue is what I would call a "detail" person. The questions started flowing.

"Does anyone have her medical records?"

"Was she cremated or buried?"

"If she was buried where is she buried?"

"What about my father in all this, is he alive, was he there when she died?"

"Why was she in a mental institution if she just had epilepsy? Was she mentally disabled?"

"Is my uncle married, does he have any kids?"

The questioning continued in her desperate hopes that there might be some little piece of information that I had gathered but had just forgotten to tell her. I think she thought that if she asked me enough questions it would trigger my memory and I could provide her with another little nugget about her mother. It wasn't working.

After giving my wife the report I was expecting to hear things like, "Thank you honey, that was so kind of you to do for me." Or, "You are my hero…you da man." Or better yet, "I owe you one and you can collect tonight." No such luck.

After I told her that all of her questioning was pointless and that maybe she should have made the call herself her response went something like, "You are so insensitive, you just don't understand me."

To which I responded, "Here's the phone number, knock yourself out." Based on my response I think she probably was right about me being insensitive but I pushed the issue anyway. For the next several days I would ask her if she had called her uncle back yet and the answer was always, "No." She wanted me to call him back but I refused, "If all this stuff is so important to you then you need to make the call."

Well, she finally made the call and spoke briefly with her Uncle Peter and then had a long conversation with his wife, her aunt. These two women started talking like they were long-lost friends. Apparently her aunt had been giving her uncle the same ear-full for the past several days. Sue's aunt was letting her uncle hear about it for not asking me any questions or even getting my name and contact in- formation when he had me on the phone. The aunt had just been hoping and praying that we would call them back. To her we were family and she wanted to get to know more about us.

Before Uncle Peter handed the phone to his wife he mentioned to Sue that he had written a book a few years earlier that involved some of their family history and he thought we might enjoy a copy. Sue gave him our address and his book arrived a few days later.

So, as it turns out, the deep dark family secrets that no one seemed to want to share with my wife and that could potentially embarrass the extended family whose social circle included the most prominent families in the Inland Northwest is this:

- Sue's father was not a good man and ran from his responsibility.

- Sue's mother was a ward of the state and a patient in a mental institution.

- Sue was born in this same mental institution, an extremely rare event and something to be hidden. Revealing such a fact might lead to questions that would prompt the embarrassing disclosure of the other two secrets.

Here it might be worth noting that had this situation occurred ten years later and Sue's mother been pregnant in a state facility, my wife would have been aborted. A rather sobering thought, at least to me.

Today I am quite confident that Sue's adoptive family would have never concealed these secrets had they known, as Paul Harvey used to say, "The rest of the story." Based on what we eventually discovered, my wife's mother, Sally was quite the heroine. These details were provided to us in the book we received from Uncle Peter and from research done by one of Sue's biological sisters.

Sally was born in 1928 and was two years older than her only sibling, Uncle Peter. Sally and Peter's father, Sue's biological grandfather, Robert Wygle was a mining engineer working at a mine near Baguio, Mountain Province, Philippine Islands when the Japanese attacked Pearl Harbor on December 7, 1941. Ten hours after the attack on Pearl Harbor the Japanese began their aerial assault of the Philippine Islands. Due to the uncertainty over the long-term intentions of the Japanese and the ability of the Americans forces to defend the Islands, the next few days were quite intense for any Americans living there.

Five days later, December 12th, General MacArthur and the American forces withdrew from the Philippines and the thousands of Americans remaining on the Islands were on their own. On December 20th, after it had become apparent that staying in the Philippines was not a good idea, Grandfather Robert loaded his wife Margaret and their two kids, Peter and Sally on a bus headed to Manila. Robert stayed behind to wrap up a few loose ends at the mine and would follow them in two or three days.

Margaret and their two children were to go to Manila and make the arrangements for the family to get on the first available vessel headed towards the USA. If there was any delay in Robert's arrival in Manila, Margaret and the kids were to leave for the USA without him and he would eventually catch up with them there. The plan seemed to be reasonable. It only took a four hour bus ride to travel the 158 miles to Manila and despite the Japanese bombings, buses were making this trip every day.

The family arrived safely in Manila on December 20th, but while Robert was still wrapping up things at the mine, on December 22nd, the Japanese invasion began at Lingayen Gulf. This invasion cut off the road between Baguio and Manila and with it all bus traffic to Manila. When Robert received word of the Japanese invasion he knew he had to get to Manila as quickly as possible. Since traveling by road would be suicidal his only option was to travel on foot, bushwhacking his way through the jungle and hoping for the best.

Robert gathered up only the bare essentials of what he could carry and headed out towards Manila. It was 125 miles to Manila as the crow flies, 158 miles by road but he knew it would be much further for him if he was to avoid being captured or killed by the Japanese.

Robert started out on horseback, but soon had to abandon the horse because of the difficult terrain and the attention a horse would draw when trying to hide.

He spent the next fifteen days on foot as he worked his way to Manila, eating and drinking whatever he could scrounge, sleeping whenever he could find a safe place and being careful to avoid being seen. He finally arrived in Manila on January 6th but had no idea whether or not his family was still there. Robert had heard that several American families were hiding out in Catholic Convents. He spent the next two days going from one Convent to another looking for his family and dodging the Japanese who were occupying Manila.

Robert, still unaware as to the whereabouts of his family was finally captured on January 8th and taken to Santo Tomas University, which had been converted to a Japanese POW (Internment) camp. This makeshift POW camp had been converted to house the 4000 plus American & British citizens found on the Philippine Islands during WWII. Later that same day the Japanese discovered the Americans hiding in the Catholic Convent. Still unaware as to the whereabouts of their husband and father, Margaret, Peter and Sally were also captured and taken to the Santo Tomas POW Camp. Robert had no idea where his family was and his family had no idea what had happened to him, but on this day, in the POW camp, the family was reunited.

I don't want to make light of the time this family spent in the POW camp; that story alone could be the subject of an entirely different book. The conditions in this camp were horrid. During their thirty-seven months of confinement the average male prisoner lost fifty-one pounds and the average female prisoner lost thirty-two pounds. Peter entered the camp at eleven years of age and Sally at thirteen. We believe it was during this time that Sally developed epilepsy that would eventually lead to her being institutionalized. Here is a brief quote from Peter's book about his sister Sally:

"She (Sally) had the durability and constitution of a Sherman tank. She, like Mom and Dad, was an incurable volunteer. When the shelling started right after we were liberated, she disappeared into the aid stations to wrap bandages and we didn't see her for days at a time."[2]

It was a good thing I called Sue's Uncle Peter when I did because he died shortly afterwards. His book revealed some things about Sally which greatly helped my wife discover her past. Her mother was ill, not crazy as many of the family had been led to believe. From copies of letters we recently obtained that were written during her final years, we also learned that even though her entire life seems relatively tragic she remained a very upbeat, caring and compassionate woman. One such letter was written the day before my wife was born. The letter was addressed to the man and woman who had earlier adopted one of Sue's older sisters. This letter pleaded with the family to adopt Sally's third child so that both children would have a sibling to grow up with.

To me Sally was quite a hero. She had two daughters that she had willingly given up for adoption and when a third arrived and her situation had gotten even worse, abortion was not an option. She did everything within her power to make certain that her baby, my wife, went to a good family that would provide her the opportunity for a life that she could not provide. The deep dark family secret turned out to be a story which my wife and I gladly tell.

---

2   *Surviving A Japanese POW Camp* by Peter Wygle p.188

REFLECTION

1) What part of Perry's story did you identify with the most?

_____

_____

_____

_____

_____

2) Describe a situation where you went out of your way to help someone and felt unappreciated.

_____

_____

_____

_____

_____

3) In what ways have you been insensitive to the feelings of others?_____

_____

_____

_____

_____

4) Describe a deep dark secret from your life that you now have freedom to talk about today.

_____

_____

_____

_____

_____

5) What do you think would be the worst things about being in a POW camp for a few years?

_____

_____

_____

_____

_____

6) In what ways has adversity made you stronger?

_____

_____

_____

_____

_____

7) In what ways is adoption a better choice than abortion?

_____

_____

_____

_____

_____

CHAPTER 13

Butt Bling

I AM A GUY. I AM a guy with a wife. Being a guy with a wife makes me a husband. That statement may seem trite but just keep reading. Even though I have been a husband to the same wife for over thirty-five years I am no closer to figuring out my wife or women in general than I was when I was single.

I also occasionally write. Some have called me a writer but the truth is I am NOT a writer; I'm a hack with a good editor. Sometimes my writing spills over into my role as husband and my role as husband spills into my writing. There are some really funny stories I could tell you involving my wife, but I have an awesome wife and a great marriage and I'd like to keep it that way. But once in a while the temptation is too much to bear.

Like most writers I secretly hope to be remembered for writing something so profound or so enlightening that I will be frequently quoted in other books and forever remembered as the author and originator of some fantastic line.

Imagine that I am seated at a table enjoying small talk over dinner with a group of other writers at a Writer's Conference in Dallas.

None of the other writers have ever heard of me before the conference and I know none of them. As we're talking about our respective works the subject comes up about being quoted and coined phrases. I'm finally asked if I had ever been quoted or if I had ever coined any phrases.

"Well, I don't know that I have ever been quoted by another writer," I reply, "but I have coined a phrase!"

"And what is that?" I'm asked.

"Butt Bling."

As soon as the words "Butt Bling" fall out of my mouth I am now compelled to tell the story…Sorry Dear.

As I said, I'm a guy, a guy with a wife. As with any guy with a wife I must continue my daily attempt to go where no man has ever gone before…into the mind of women.

Understanding the mind of a man is quite simple. A woman can ask her husband what he is thinking and if he says, "Nothing," men know that there is a really good chance that he indeed is telling the truth. You see with men our minds can idle. Sometimes we're like the driver sitting at a green traffic signal after the light has changed. We might look like we're headed somewhere, but nothing is going to happen until someone honks at us. At times there really is NOTHING going on in there. Every man knows that heavenly place that we affectionately call "ZONED OUT."

But with women it's different. With women there is always a whirlwind of activity going on in their heads. The number of different things they think about, all at the same time seems endless.

I've heard one comedian use a Windows computer operating system to explain the difference between men and women. Men will only have one window open at any given time. When they are done they close that window and open another window or just shut off the computer. With women the computer is ALWAYS on and they may have ten or more windows open at any given time. Some windows never close and rarely are tasks completed before another window is opened. A window may stay open for days, weeks or even years before being closed.

To reiterate, if you ask a man what he is thinking and he tells you, "Nothing," there is a strong likelihood that he is telling the truth. But women don't get that – how can anyone possibly be thinking of nothing? Then, of course, there are times when we really *are* thinking of something, but it's just easier to say that we're thinking of "nothing" than to disclose what is really going on in there. We say "nothing" because we don't want to endure the inevitable fallout that would result from telling the truth. You know what I mean. Can you imagine my wife asking me what I was thinking and instead of saying, "Nothing," I said, "Maybe I shouldn't have eaten that sixth burrito for breakfast."

Women are totally different. If I asked my wife what she was thinking and she said "nothing" she would now have my full attention. For her to think about "nothing" is indeed quite impossible. I don't know much, but one thing I do know is that "nothing" is code for "I'm really pissed-off at you."

Even though I know that it is quite impossible for me to figure out my wife, as a husband I am compelled to make the effort. One day I noticed my wife wearing blue jeans that had this ornate, metallic, matching design on both rear pockets. I had recently noticed other women wearing similar types of jeans so I thought it was a new fad or something. I'm the last person on this planet that would have any interest or knowledge of women's clothing fashions, but seeing these jeans on her sparked my curiosity just a bit.

"So, what's with the Butt Bling?" I asked.

I had never heard the phrase "Butt Bling"; I had just made it up on the fly. Although my question may in *"hindsight"* seem ill-advised, it was sincere. I was trying to get inside my wife's head and understand the purpose of ornamental metallic objects attached to her butt. Maybe I needed some Butt Bling of my own to complete my clothing ensemble.

To me Butt Bling is kind of like a woman wearing a very nice necklace just slightly suspended above her cleavage while her upper body parts are about to fall out of her shirt. If she is trying to draw attention to her physical attributes the necklace is superfluous. If she is trying to draw attention to her necklace…well that ain't gonna happen, at least until she properly puts a shirt on.

When I asked about the Butt Bling my wife knew exactly what I was asking about. She turned, put her hands on her hips and cocked her head so that she was looking at me over the top of her glasses. "Excuse Me," she said, but in that tone that screams, "You are such an idiot." Trying to explain my reason for the question just made matters worse.

"Honey, I'm not saying the Butt Bling is good or bad. I've never seen you wearing pants like that before and I'm just trying to understand the purpose. Is the purpose to *attract* attention to your back side or is the purpose to *detract* people from staring at your back side by focusing on the bling? I'm just curious!"

She did not need to say a word; her body language said it all. In a feeble attempt to recover and remove my foot from my mouth I sheepishly consoled, "Well ya know, if the purpose of Butt Bling is to *attract* attention you're wasting your money, you don't need any help attracting attention; you have a really nice butt."

My wife turned and walked away. She never answered my question. I have no idea what ever happened to those jeans but I never saw them on her again.

REFLECTION

1) What part of Perry's story did you identify with the most?

_____

_____

_____

_____

_____

2) If married, how would you describe your relationship with your wife?_____

_____

_____

_____

_____

3) In what ways is your wife wired differently than you?

_____

_____

_____

_____

_____

4) If married, in what ways are you intentional about bringing happiness to your wife?

_____

_____

_____

_____

_____

5) If married or divorced, in what ways could you make or have made your marriage better?

_____

_____

_____

_____

_____

6) If unmarried, what qualities should you look for in a wife?

_____

_____

_____

_____

_____

7) What advice would you give to someone considering marriage?

_____

_____

_____

_____

_____

CHAPTER 14

Opening the Vault

OF ALL THE STUPID AND embarrassing things I've done in my life there has been one thing that has been the granddaddy of all my embarrassments. I have never wanted to talk about it and there are only a few people who even know about it. I had conveniently packed this story away in a box and shoved that box into the deepest darkest corner of my man vault where I hoped it would never be discovered or spoken of again. I'm sharing this story with you now for reasons you'll understand at the end.

Let me start off by setting the stage. I graduated from college in 1981 with a dual major, Accounting and Business Administration. My fiancée and I went through our graduation ceremony at two o'clock in the afternoon and then were married at seven o'clock that same evening. Our wedding was a quaint ceremony in her parents' back yard.

My wife's brother provided us with a Honeymoon Suite at the Red Lion Hotel in Boise, Idaho. We were dirt poor college students with only a few meager furnishings and a few hundred dollars that had been given to us as wedding gifts. The day following our graduation and marriage in Nampa, Idaho we packed our possessions into our car and headed off to live in Grand Junction, Colorado.

We had no real honeymoon but that didn't matter. I was so ready to be done with college. I had always been entrepreneurial and was excited to get out there, make my mark and my fortune. We would have plenty of time and money for honeymooning later.

At this time the national economy was not doing very well but one of our nation's few economic bright spots was Western Colorado where I had grown up and where we now lived. The economy there was booming. The reason behind the boom was an industrial operation located in Parachute, Colorado where the Exxon Corporation, with the assistance of Federal subsidies, had invested millions of dollars to develop the technology to turn oil shale (rocks) into marketable oil. Money was flowing and I was confident we were in the right place at the right time.

Fresh out of college, my wife and I were hired by a local businessman to manage a community of apartments known as Sunrise Gardens, a new development of eighteen four-unit buildings. I handled the business side and any maintenance issues and my wife handled any cleaning required with an occasional vacancy. These were brand new units and because of the booming economy we had a waiting list of tenants ready to move in as soon as their unit was finished.

May 2, 1982, less than a year after our graduation and wedding date is a day that will be forever branded in the minds of those who lived in that area at that time. "Black Sunday" as locals came to call it, is the day when hundreds of employees showed up for work at the Exxon facility only to find the gates locked. Without any sort of warning Exxon pulled the plug on the oil shale development and left thousands of people out of work. Grand Junction, the largest city in the area, had been flourishing for several years and now found itself dealing with an economic bust and with it massive unemployment and the accompanying social woes.

I'm not sure who started it, it may have been the local newspaper, but a popular phrase at the time was, "Whoever is the last person to leave Grand Junction please turn out the lights." Real estate prices dropped in half almost overnight and new neighborhoods that had sprung up out of the boom were now ghost towns. I could tell you story upon story about people I knew who were personally devastated, but nothing I could write would adequately described the heartache and despair experienced within that community.

The apartments we were managing were also impacted by the economy. When we started we had dozens of inquiries each day and a waiting list of people who needed a home. We were getting premium rents. Less than a year later we had a fifty percent vacancy rate and were offering two months' free rent as an enticement for new tenants. The businessman we worked for owned hundreds of highly leveraged properties and eventually committed suicide.

During this time the mortgage industry was loosely regulated. Anyone with a Veteran (VA) or Federal Housing Authority (FHA) loan on their home could have someone else assume their loan without the buyer needing to qualify. In other words, any Tom, Dick or Harry could walk in off the street and take over someone else's VA or FHA loan regardless of their ability to make the payments. These types of loans made up about half of the mortgages on homes at this time and people were so desperate to sell their homes that these "non-qualifying assumptions" were commonplace.

At the age of twenty-four I started buying property and by the time I was twenty-six I owned dozens of properties. These properties were extremely easy to buy and I was confident that the market would eventually come back to the price levels seen before the bust. I figured as long as I could rent them for enough to make the payments that my wealth would grow through principle reduction (tenants making my payments) and market appreciation. Cash-flow was very tight but the plan was working and it seemed as if I could do no wrong. I was becoming a legend, at least a legend in my own mind.

Pride goes before the fall.

Among the properties that I owned was a mobile home subdivision located on the opposite side of the state in the little town of Sterling. This subdivision brought in over seven thousand dollars each month, a great deal of money in 1985 but the cash flow was just barely keeping up with my payments and expenses. The beautiful thing about this mobile home subdivision was that it was over half vacant when I bought it so the upside potential was huge.

One day I got a call from a real estate broker named Dan. Dan had investor contacts that had been involved in mobile home financing. And with the way the economy was these investors were foreclosing on more mobile homes than they knew what to do with. Dan's plan was to set up these foreclosed mobile homes in my mobile home subdivision and either rent or sell these mobile homes to fill up the vacant lots in my subdivision. The investors provided the mobile home, I provided the lots to set them on and Dan would find buyers for these homes and lease their lot from us. It seemed like a very viable plan with no downside.

Dan and I worked out a deal where he would take control and management of the mobile home subdivision which included collecting the rents and paying the operating expenses. He agreed to pay me $5000 per month and each year my monthly payment would escalate as he filled the subdivision. The initial $5000 per month was just enough to cover my payments on the property and as time went by the arrangement would certainly provide me with a nice monthly income. The attorneys prepared an exhaustive contract and we were on our way.

Everything worked splendidly for the first couple of months, but Dan's payments started getting later and later each month which in turn caused me to be late on my payments each month. I would call Dan and ask when he planned on making his payment and he would always tell me whatever I wanted to hear. It was at this point that I learned a very valuable lesson: *if a man's word is worthless his signature is just as worthless.*

To make a long story short, Dan's promises turned out to be lies and the payments stopped altogether. I was still obligated to make my payments but Dan was now in control of my property. This nightmare dragged on for months while my payments got further and further behind.

I took Dan to court and won a substantial judgement against him but I never saw a penny of the money he owed. For me it was too little, too late. I had been robbing Peter to pay Paul for months and I was now behind on all of my loans. I owed money to several Banks and S&L companies. There was one S&L that I owed over two million dollars to when I devised a plan that would allow me to catch up on my payments. But their hands were tied and they were unable to work with me. Due to the real estate bust this S&L was also in deep trouble and the FDIC was in the process of taking them over.

I tried everything imaginable to salvage my empire but as it turned out, at the age of twenty-seven, I had no choice but to file bankruptcy. That's right. It is now out of the vault and out of the box. IN 1986 I FILED FOR BANKRUPTCY. Fortunately, my bankruptcy did not involve my wife and I was able to keep the bankruptcy fairly well hidden.

For the next thirty years people knew me for my business acumen and I took great pride in this. My entire identity had been wrapped up in my business reputation and my business know-how. The bankruptcy happened when I was still very young and relatively unknown. But as I grew older and became more well-known the pressure to keep the bankruptcy secret intensified. Maybe it is true that I could have legitimately passed the blame of my failure onto someone else, but for thirty years I was extremely shameful of the fact that I had indeed failed.

To many this shame that I've felt may seem ridiculous, but there are also many who will understand. The shame was very real. I remember being out with some very close friends who were having some financial struggles. Thinking that she was comforting them my wife very casually mentioned my bankruptcy. I was quietly steaming for the next couple of hours and then let her have it with both barrels as soon as we were alone. "Don't you EVER tell ANYBODY about that," I demanded.

From where I sit today I can look back and say that my shame and my attitude were indeed ridiculous. Even though the experience was deeply painful there was much I learned from it. And I believe I became a much more cautious and conservative individual as a result. I also believe that if I had not failed at that point in my life it would have happened sooner or later. I was much too cocky and over-confident in my abilities. This would have caught up with me eventually.

I have come to believe that I could have never fulfilled God's plan and purpose for my life if I had not been through this humbling experience. I wonder how I might have been able to use my story to help other men experiencing similar financial hardship. But in my pride I remained silent and let them suffer on their own.

Today I speak less and listen more. I'm more understanding and less judgmental. I'm less selfish and more generous. I've learned that life has its ups and downs and even when things seem their darkest there are still reasons to be thankful.

REFLECTION

1) What part of Perry's story did you identify with the most?

---

2) In what ways do you struggle with pride?

---

3) Describe ways that you have been affected by materialism

---

4) How comfortable are you with having debt?

---

5) In what ways do you share your wealth in an attempt to help others less fortunate? _____

_____

_____

_____

_____

6) What changes do you need to make in the way you manage money?_____

_____

_____

_____

_____

7) Who do you trust that you will share these answers with and will hold you accountable to make the changes you've listed?

_____

_____

_____

_____

_____

CHAPTER 15

Terry Canfield

MY WORK REQUIRES A GREAT deal of reading, writing and meetings. I have found that coffee shops serve as an excellent venue where I can schedule several appointments throughout the day and still read and write between these appointments. On days where I have no appointments I enjoy working from my home office but that happens only one or two days a week. I have my favorite hangouts and try to arrange my schedule so that I can stay at the same coffee shop for several hours at a time.

The day I met Terry Canfield was no different than hundreds of days before but I remember that day well. I was sitting by myself working on my laptop at a table in a corner of my favorite coffee shop. I looked up from my work and made eye contact with another man seated at another nearby table. I knew this man by name but he is not someone that I would say that I know well. His name is Rob. Across the room Rob and I gave each other one of those nods as if to say, "Hey, how's it going."

Rob was sitting far enough away that the head nod acknowledgement was appropriate yet he was siting closed enough that I noticed that he had a copy of the book *Webmertise* sitting on the table in front of him. In case you're not familiar with the book *Webmertise* I'll tell you a little bit about it because it is relevant to this story.

Webmertise...A Small Business Guide to Internet Marketing is a book that I wrote in 2012 when I was still doing Marketing Consulting work. This book was written for small business owners and leaders of organizations that are large enough to have an advertising/ marketing budget yet small enough not to have a knowledgeable marketing professional on their payroll. Small business and organizational leaders usually get their marketing advice from someone who is trying to sell them something or from an ad agency paid on commission, which is just as bad. Marketing and advertising advice should not be trusted if your advisor is paid based on how much you spend. Enough said; I'd better not get started on that subject.

Anyway, it is not often that I see someone in a coffee shop reading one of the books that I've written. It is so unusual that seeing Rob with a copy *Webmertise* in front of him really made that encounter memorable.

Within a couple of minutes of Rob and my mutual nods, a man I would guess to be in his mid to upper fifties joined Rob at his table and I went back to work. I didn't give the situation another thought.

About an hour later, the man who had joined Rob walked up to my table holding Rob's copy of *Webmertise.* He politely excused himself for interrupting me and explained that Rob had loaned him his copy of my book and that Rob had pointed me out as the author. He introduced himself as Terry Canfield and asked if I had a couple of minutes. He went on to explain that he was about to launch a new business and asked if I would be willing to schedule an appointment with him to give him some pointers on how to best market the launch of this business.

It is important to note that at this point in my life I was winding down my marketing consulting business to plunge full-time into the task of developing a non-profit organization named Abortion Anonymous (AbAnon). Terry had asked for a meeting but I know where these meetings tend to end up. I had absolutely no interest in meeting with Terry to talk about his new business and I certainly didn't want to take on another consulting client. While smiling politely I told Terry that I was no longer doing marketing consultations and that I had recently experienced a major change of direction for my life. I was carefully guarding what that new direction actually was because I never know what kind of reaction I'll get when the word "abortion" is mentioned.

Rather than humbly accepting my rejection of his request and walking away Terry threw a curve at me when he asked, "So what are you doing now?"

Being a bit deliberate I responded, "Well, it's complicated." I then went on to explain how I had recently established a non-profit organization and that its purpose is to help women and men recover from the emotional pain that inevitably results from their involvement in an abortion.

As I explained my involvement in abortion healing programs Terry became acutely interested in what I was saying. Over the next few minutes we had a great conversation about AbAnon. He was fully engaged in what I had to say. He asked me several questions in response to the things I had just explained about the adverse effects of abortion on women and men. He was very affirming about what I was doing and thanked me for having the courage to start such an organization.

I must have gained Terry's trust in those few minutes. Although he hesitated for just a moment, Terry opened up to me. "When I was in my twenties my girlfriend and I had an abortion," he confessed. "Everything you just said about abortion is right on; you just described us to a tee."

What Terry did not know was that I was doing some research and in the process of gathering information about the effects of abortion on men. I had already interviewed a handful of men but I needed more stories for the men's book I would be writing for AbAnon. The tables had just been turned and I'm certain that I was now more interested in making an appointment with Terry than he was with me. I really wanted to hear his story. We set an appointment to meet the following week.

For Terry to open up to me so quickly was unusual. My experience has been that men are very slow to open up about their involvement in an abortion. Men seem to stuff their abortion experience in a box and shove that box into the deepest darkest corner of their man vault, never to be opened again.

Women, on the other hand, are quite different. Whenever women hear that I'm in the abortion healing business many must think I'm safe. Abortion is such a private, intimate and spiritual topic. At first I was surprised at how often women would open up to me, a complete stranger, but women tell me their stories ALL THE TIME. It happens so often that I've gotten used to it but I admit that I was a bit uncomfortable the first few times it happened.

The more I talk with men the more I am convinced that men are no different than women when it comes to processing their abortion. Just as with women, no man can be involved in an abortion without being adversely affected by it. But the strange thing is that most men don't seem to be able to connect the dots between their abortion experience and the destructive behavior they use to medicate their pain.

Rarely do men open up and it's even rarer to have them do so quickly. But Terry Canfield was different; he opened up his man vault to me right away and held nothing back. He shared with me some other things that he wished he had done differently as well. Terry was refreshingly transparent. We met two or three more times. I gave Terry marketing advice for his business and he gave me his abortion story.

I have heard dozens maybe even hundreds of abortion stories, but when I interview people as part of my research it is much more involved. When people tell me their abortion story it can easily take a couple of hours. As a writer, the trick is taking these two hour stories and write them so that they can be read or told in three or four minutes. Much or their story must be left out, hopefully with minimal loss of the raw emotion behind it. It is like trying to tell the life story of some great leader like Abraham Lincoln or William Wilberforce in a two hour movie. There is always so much more to a person's life than we can possibly see or understand.

After going back and forth with the editing of his story, Terry finally gave his permission to use it, but he had one condition. There was someone Terry needed to talk to first.

There is a great deal of Terry's story that I cannot share because it was his wish that his story not bring shame or embarrassment to the other people involved. At the end of his story Terry briefly mentions his daughter. Terry told me that he had not been a very good father to his daughter. And other than his involvement in two abortions, his strained relationship with his daughter was his biggest regret in life.

Part of Terry's story is that Terry had never mentioned anything to his daughter about her siblings that he and her mother had aborted. He also believed that the mother of this daughter had never broached the subject with her either. Before his story was put "out there" Terry wanted to tell his daughter his abortion story himself to be sure that she would not be blindsided if and when his story became public. I encouraged Terry to contact his daughter as soon as possible. It was obvious that his relationship with his daughter was tearing him up inside.

Terry's desire to mend his relationship with his daughter was evident; he contacted her immediately after our meeting. After waiting a few days, I contacted Terry to see if he had met with his daughter yet, and if so, how did the meeting turn out? He had indeed met with his daughter, but the meeting had not gone as well as he had hoped. He told me that he still had a lot of work to do. Terry never blamed anyone else for his failures. He took full responsibility for the state of this relationship and was fully committed to do everything necessary to mend it.

Thursday, May 21, 2015 Terry and I had coffee together for the final time. When I came home from work on Friday of the following week my wife asked me if I had heard about the family that had been murdered about ten miles from where we live. My wife was concerned that there was a murderer on the loose and wanted my assurances that we were not in any danger, which to her is a completely rational concern. I assured her that she had nothing to worry about and thought nothing more about it.

We were sitting in our living room after dinner that evening and she just couldn't seem to let go of her "murderer in our neighborhood" concern and started reading to me a news article from her iPhone. The following is a portion of the article from the May 29, 2015 Spokesman Review:

Investigators sift and search through debris Thursday at the Colbert home where three bodies were found in the aftermath of a fire.

Investigators seek leads

Investigators believe the suspect or suspects might have left the area and tried to dispose of evidence. They ask that citizens report suspicious people or vehicles, or items with smoke or fire damage that look like they've been dumped.

Spokane County detectives believe a fire department lieutenant, his wife and her adult son were shot to death, (and) then whoever did it set fire to the family's home to destroy evidence of the crime.

The county Medical Examiner's Office has identified the victims as Spokane Fire Lt. Terry Canfield, 59; Lisa M. Canfield, 52; and John Robert Constable, 23.

Terry Canfield was a 28-year veteran of the Spokane Fire Department and lived at the home at 20 E. Chattaroy Road.

As soon as my wife read the name Terry Canfield I stopped her to make certain I had heard her correctly. I told her that I knew Terry well and that we had just met for coffee a few days earlier. He was scheduled to have shoulder surgery the Friday following our last meeting and I had even sent him an email on the day he was killed asking him how his shoulder surgery had gone.

Terry had confided in me that his two greatest desires were to reconcile with his daughter and that his abortion story would be used to help other men and women keep from experiencing the same pain and regret that he had. I do not know Terry's daughter but my hope is that this book finds its way into her hands and that she sees her dad, not for who he had been, but for who he had become. May you meet him again in heaven!

Here is Terry's abortion story.

My story is one that I believe possibly millions of men can relate to. I grew up in a middle-class family; my father had served in the military and provided for our family by working a blue-collar job most of his working years. I was the youngest of four children including a much older half-sister from my mother's first marriage. My parents taught us the value of giving back to our community, themselves being foster parents for a dozen or so children throughout the years, even adopting a fifth child when I was in my teens.

Like any family, we were far from perfect, but I think people viewed our family as "good people." We attended church semi-regularly and I was baptized as a child. My moral compass may not have been set on true north but it was pointing generally in the right direction.

As I grew out of my teenage years and into my twenties I gradually moved away from what I knew in my heart to be right. Basically what I was taught as a child was not strong enough to suppress my raging hormones, a common malady with young men.

In my mid-twenties I began a career in Fire Service and met a gal during EMT training. After dating a few months we moved in together. She was a few years older than I and brought a six-year-old son and a nine-year-old daughter into the relationship. Our relationship was not a strong one; it lacked commitment on my part. For me our relationship was one of convenience: I provided her the emotional and child-rearing support she needed and she provided what I needed.

After living together for about a year she discovered that she was preg-nant and informed me that she had made the decision to abort the child. Who could blame her? She already had two kids and was in the physical testing phase as she prepared for a job in public protective services. But I think the true reason for her aborting our child was that she felt trapped – no way out. She was pregnant with a third child and I didn't offer any support or encouragement of any kind. In other words, she had no confidence in our relationship and I said nothing, neglecting my God-given duty to take responsibility for my actions and to be the protector of my family.

After the abortion I remember feeling guilty about it…I knew that what we had done was wrong. I say "we" because deep within my soul, even though it was her decision, I failed to stop it when I had the power to do so.

A year later and newly hired at a job she had spent years training for, she was pregnant again. Unfortunately nothing had changed within me or within our relationship. This time we both decided to abort the child. The guilt I was carrying was not yet bad enough to change my behavior.

After the second abortion I couldn't stand it any longer… I wanted out and I told her so. She was devastated. She tried to kill herself by taking a lethal dose of very powerful medication. Thanks to my medical training I recognized what was happening and rushed her to the ER in the middle of the night; only minutes away from dying, the team at the ER got her through it.

We never talked about it, but I can't help but think that the two abortions had something to do with her mental state. The abortions certainly affected mine. I attempted to break up again but this attempt also failed. Looking back maybe I should have just walked away, but I couldn't just leave her after all we'd been through. However I did take off for a month, basically I had to get away for a while. During that month I was constantly stoned or drunk.

Eventually we parted ways and each of us moved on with our lives.

Around age thirty-eight I started attending church again in an attempt to fill the huge hole in my heart. I can't say that I've ever had one of those "God encounters." But several friends and Pastors have prayed with me, asking God to forgive me for my role in these abortions and for many other things I've done. I'm still a work in progress but I know that my moral compass is once again generally pointing in the right direction.

I don't think about my involvement with the two abortions every day. I know that I'm forgiven, but those abortions still sit at the top of the heap of my own condemnation. In retrospect, I wonder how I could ever have gotten to the point where my own selfishness had caused me to lose my spiritual, emotional and physiological perspective to the point where I was willing to kill my own children.

As a paramedic I'm in the life-saving business. I know what I did and there is no intellectually honest way to rationalize it. Except for my daughter, there is nothing that I wouldn't give to go back and change what I've done. And I hope that by telling my story I may be able to save others from suffering from the same regret and shame as I have.

Terry Canfield

REFLECTION

1) What part of Perry's story did you identify with the most?

_____

_____

_____

_____

2) How would you describe your opinions regarding abortion?

_____

_____

_____

_____

3) How has abortion affected your life and family?

_____

_____

_____

_____

4) Perry states that no man can be involved in an abortion without being adversely affected by it and that most men are unable to make the connection between their abortion experience and the destructive behavior they use to medicate their pain. To what extent do you find this statement to be true or untrue in your own life or with people you know?

_____

_____

_____

_____

5) In Terry's story he says that he neglected his "God-given duty to take responsibility for my actions and to be the protector of my family." In what ways do you agree or disagree with this statement?

_____

_____

_____

_____

_____

6) What would you tell a friend whose wife, girlfriend or daughter was contemplating having an abortion?

_____

_____

_____

_____

_____

7) Who comes to mind as being someone with whom you need to repair a relationship? What action will you take? Who will you ask to hold you accountable to take this action?

_____

_____

_____

_____

_____

NOTE: On the subject of abortion it is recommended that you read another book written by Perry Underwood, *Change the Shame*.

CHAPTER 16

The No Hitter

IN MAJOR LEAGUE BASEBALL THE definition of a "Perfect Game" is a game in which all the batters from one team are retired in order, with no one reaching base. In almost 140 years of Major League Baseball which includes over 200,000 games played, there have been only twenty-three perfect games, and even as great as some pitchers have been, no single pitcher has ever thrown more than one. Pitching a perfect game is extremely rare.

The next best achievement for a pitcher is to pitch a "No-hitter" which is defined as a game in which a pitcher or pitchers complete a game of nine innings or more without allowing a hit. No-hitters are about twelve times more common than perfect games but still a relatively difficult accomplishment. At the time of this writing the powers that be have recognized 294 no-hitters throughout professional baseball history.

I was a fairly decent baseball player in my younger days but never a pitcher; my position was short-stop. But if I had been a pitcher I believe that I would approach every game with the hope of pitching a perfect game. Once the chance of pitching the perfect game was gone I would then alter my hopes to where I would now hope to pitch a no-hitter. Once the chance of pitching a no-hitter was gone I would alter my hopes to where I would now hope to pitch a shutout. Once the chance of pitching a shutout was gone I would alter my hopes to where I would now hope to earn the win. Once the chance of winning seemed to be slipping away I would alter my hopes to where I would now hope to minimize the damage and do what I could to prevent the opposing team from scoring any more runs. Beyond that I think I would hope that everyone would just simply forget about the game.

The point of all this is to give you a glimpse into my competitive nature as I approach every situation hoping to make the best of it. If a situation changes then my hopes change so that I will continue to pursue the most desirable remaining outcome. Rather than whining and complaining about dashed hopes I choose to evaluate the situation and adjust my hopes to the then current best possible scenario. Notice that I said that I adjust my "hopes" rather than "expectations," which is totally different and would be an unhealthy approach to adversity.

For you baseball players…here comes the change-up.

When we lived in Alaska the church we attended was located in South Anchorage but we lived about thirty minutes away in Eagle River. This was a very large church so there were many families like ours that traveled some distance to attend this church each Sunday; many were from the Eagle River area. Because there were so many families living in the Eagle River area my wife hosted a weekly Bible Study in our home for women who lived there. One of the women who attended my wife's Bible Study lived in our neighborhood just a few doors down the street from us. I'll call her Barbie, which is not her real name.

Barbie's husband was about 6'4", had a muscular build, was a Colonel/Surgeon in the Air Force and was quite handsome. When I say handsome what I mean is that I would love to have his build and his looks. I'll call the husband Ken, which is not his real name either. Ken was an Orthopedic Surgeon and worked at the military hospital in the Anchorage area. He was the complete package. He was one of those guys that we average guys love to hate.

Ken and Barbie had the picture perfect family and had what appeared to be the picture perfect life. Not only was Barbie beautiful but she was educated and trained as a dentist. Because Ken had a great job she had the choice of pursuing her career or being a stay-home mom. Barbie chose to put her career on hold and to invest her life into raising their two darling girls.

Barbie confided in my wife that she and Ken were going through some marital struggles. She had discovered that Ken was having an affair with a woman at work and unfortunately, this had not been the first time. My wife shared this information with me because Barbie was hoping that I could befriend Ken and talk some sense into him. Even though we attended the same church and lived on the same street I barely knew Ken but I initiated a friendship in hopes of helping a brother. Ken and I met a few times for breakfast or coffee, but it didn't take long to figure out that our relationship was lopsided; only one of us was making any real effort to maintain this relationship and it wasn't Ken.

One thing about close relationships is that both people have to want it for them to work. This has been a hard lesson for me to learn. I am blessed to have several very close friends but in each of these relationships both parties are intentional about spending quality time together. I believe that men need strong relationships with other men almost as much as we need food and water. Yet so many men I know have no really strong friendships. To me this is quite sad. But just like being good at your profession or playing golf, to be good at having friendships takes practice; it takes time; and it requires being intentional about it.

Some guys can forget their wife's birthday and that alone is all that their wife needs to feel justified in divorcing the bum, but not Barbie. Ken had engaged in multiple affairs and she was once again ready to truly forgive him and do everything necessary to hold their picture perfect family together. Ken promised that he would never stray again and when he and I met he was always contrite and said exactly the things he was supposed to say.

It wasn't long after Ken's most recent promise of fidelity that Ken brought home another female coworker to spend the night while Barbie and the girls were out of town. As smart as Ken is…he is a fool. If my calling Ken a fool offends you then please accept my apology. You might also want to read Solomon's Proverbs and ask yourself if the shoe fits…Just sayin'.

It happened again and again and each time Ken seemed contrite and promised that this affair would be his last. I don't know where Ken and Barbie are today but they are not together. I heard that Barbie finally divorced the guy and she and the two daughters moved back to where she grew up.

Ken had the life that 99.9% of the other men on this planet wish they had. But Ken's life was still missing something; there was a void in his heart. Ken tried to fill his void by having sex with as many women as he could get away with. It didn't work. He forced out of his life the people he loved most and his void became even bigger.

So how does this happen? How can a man who "has it all" throw it all away for momentary gratification? In asking this I'm not referring to the majority of men in this world. When you get right down to it most men live their lives pursuing whatever they think will make them "happy." For men with misaligned values happiness is found on the other side of a zipper. We know that without Christ men are selfish beings who live only to gratify themselves in whatever manner they think they can get away with. But how is it that "Christian" men who know right from wrong, profess to be living according to biblical teachings, find themselves having affairs?

Let's be real here. We are men and none of us are exempt from temptation but sexual temptation is far different than actually going through with it and having an affair. I would suggest that to find a man who has gone through life without ever experiencing sexual temptation would be about as rare as pitching the perfect game in baseball. When it comes to sexual temptation, I'm not convinced that spending one's life in a Monastery would significantly increase a man's chances of pitching a perfect game. The opportunity to act on the temptation may be removed, but temptation still remains. So the next best thing would be a no-hitter. Let me explain.

I have a friend whom I'll call him John who would frequently tell me about the women that would "come on" to him. To my knowledge John has never been unfaithful to his wife. But I've known John for many years and, if his stories are true, women coming on to him happens with frequent regularity. I would describe John as being average in just about every way: average height, average weight, average intelligence, average income, average looks and so forth. About the only thing that John excels in is his profession. So to some he might appear extremely intelligent if one only knows him within the context of his workplace. After hearing John tell me about some come-on for the umpteenth time I couldn't help but wonder, "What's wrong with me?"

While I'll admit that when it comes to the measurements of a man I am nothing special. With the exception of John's expertise in his chosen profession and the fact that he definitely is a kinder person than I am, I think I would score higher than John in every category listed earlier. Compared to John I am taller, more fit, just as intelligent, make a decent living, have a full (but thinning) head of hair and definitely better looking. But I NEVER have women coming on to me. While I probably should have viewed this irregularity as a good thing I did not. When I realized that average John was constantly being hit on and that I NEVER was hit upon it was an affront to my pride and my ego. What could it possibly be?

After this realization had been eating at me for a while the topic of flirting and infidelity came up in a conversation that included my wife, myself and a few other married couple friends. I shared with the group that I had a friend who was constantly getting hit on and that I could not understand why it never happened to me, not that I wanted it to (yeah right), but it just seemed strange to me. One of the women in the group made the suggestion that I was indeed being hit on but that I was just too naïve to recognize it. I assured her that there was NO WAY that her suggestion was true and that I would DEFINITELY know if I was being hit on.

Another woman in the group offered her opinion. She began explaining that in interactions between men and women there are very subtle sexual signals being sent that are consciously or subconsciously intended to encourage or invite response. When a woman comes on to a man she is reacting to signals being sent by the man and vice versa. She went on to say, "It's not a bad thing, as a matter of fact it's a good thing, but I've known you long enough and well enough that you don't send those subtle signals. Women don't hit on you, not because you're some homely weirdo, but because you're not sending them any signals that encourage them to do so." This friend's comments scored me some major points with my wife.

I think there is a great deal of truth in what our friend said, at least I've convinced myself that there is because it moved me from "loser" status to "hero" status. And that thought is much more palatable than to think that women find me dislikable. Using my baseball analogy, I wasn't allowing any hits because I wasn't throwing any hittable pitches.

Not long after this conversation a woman hit my fastball at my head so hard that I had to duck to keep from major injury.

I was at a Real Estate Conference with hundreds of other Real Estate Brokers from across the nation. After attending these conferences year after year I started developing casual friendships with other Brokers, both men and women, whom I would see only at these conferences. Conventions and conferences are an easy place for people looking for trouble to find it. It seems that at every conference there is a huge party on the first night where there is awesome food, dancing and enough alcohol to float a battleship. I don't dance or drink but I would generally go to these parties for the food and because I had nothing better to do.

There was this woman whom I had met at previous conventions who had always been friendly and conversant but nothing more. I remember her being attractive, a little pudgy and well endowed. On this particular evening this woman may have had a few too many adult beverages. She was waaay too friendly. She was so friendly that I asked a second female friend to stay close to me because the first woman was making me feel extremely awkward, to say the least. I knew that the second woman was "safe." I'd known her for several years and I knew her husband. It was also helpful knowing that her husband was at the convention but had decided to stay in their hotel room and avoid the party.

After the big party, where woman number one had continuously but unsuccessfully tried to drag me onto the dance floor, it was still early so eight to ten of us decided to do a walk through the Downtown area of the host city. We spent about an hour walking around and I was walking with these two women, one on each side of me. I was trying to be a polite gentleman to both of them as they scrimmaged for my attention but for different reasons.

Woman number two, my protector, finally said that her husband was probably starting to wonder where she was so she needed to head back to her room. I saw her departure as my cue to call it a night as well. I was one of the speakers at the conference and really wanted to review my presentation one final time before heading to bed.

"Well, I probably should head back to my room and go to bed," I said.

Just as I said this woman number one grabbed me by the arm, pulling me into her breasts she whispered in my ear, "Sounds good to me."

I must have turned beet red. There was no doubt what she was referring to and it was something I was totally unprepared for. "Well um," I stuttered. "I'm very flattered and it sure is a tempting offer but I really need to prepare for my presentation tomorrow." Quickly saying goodnight to the rest of the party I escorted woman number two back to the hotel where her husband was waiting in the lobby and I settled into my room, alone, for the evening.

I had been tested and I had passed. But immediately after walking away from that situation I will admit that the thoughts of what could have happened would not leave my mind that entire night. Thinking about the woman's offer combined with being in a time zone four hours earlier and the metal gymnastics that accompany a huge presentation, I hardly slept at all that night. Looking back many years later I am so glad I did the right thing.

In reflection as to why woman never seem to come on to me I discovered that the theories of both of my friends had some truth to them. I also discovered that neither of their theories was bullet-proof. I indeed recognized when I was being hit on yet I also discovered that my first friend's theory about me being a bit naïve had some truth to it.

I think the theory of my second friend, about men and women sending subtle sexual signals, is also true. But I don't think that it was true in this case; as a matter of fact I installed the safeguard of a second woman, but the advances from woman number one were there anyway. Looking back my vision is much better. I probably should have disappeared at the first hint of a problem but by hanging around I gave her an opportunity to get a hit.

Yes, I may have missed pitching the no-hitter, but I'm still in the running for a shutout.

REFLECTION

1) What part of Perry's story did you identify with the most?

_____

_____

_____

_____

_____

2) In what ways do you struggle with sexual temptation?

_____

_____

_____

_____

_____

3) To what extent would you say that the "sexual signaling" theory is relevant in your life?

_____

_____

_____

_____

_____

4) In Proverbs 4:23 King Solomon warns us, "Above all else, guard your heart." What does this mean to you?

_____

_____

_____

_____

_____

5) What specific things do you need to do to "guard your heart" from sexual temptation?"

_____

_____

_____

_____

_____

6) Create a mental list of women you know that present or could present a sexual temptation for you?

_____

_____

_____

_____

_____

7) Who do you trust that you could share your mental list with and that will hold you accountable to do the things necessary to guard your heart?

_____

_____

_____

_____

_____

CHAPTER 17

The Family Meeting

EVERY FAMILY IS DYSFUNCTIONAL IN one way or another and growing up, mine was no different. We children were constantly fighting. Sure, we loved each other; we just had peculiar ways of showing it. My older brother was teasing me one time and told me that I was adopted. My reply was, "I certainly hope so." But as much pain and hurt as we inflicted upon each other we were always there for each other when life's big storms came our way.

Even after writing this story I debated with myself whether or not I should include it in this book. I don't mind sharing my failures and embarrassing moments, but when the failure is someone else's failure it is another matter. It becomes even more complicated when that someone else is someone very close to me; someone I dearly love and respect; someone who played a significant role in developing me into who I am. That someone is my hero. That someone is my Dad.

I don't know what it is with parents, they all seem to follow the same pattern, and I as a parent was no exception. Like most parents when their children are very young my parents were really quite smart.

And as smart as my parents were it seemed that year after year they got even smarter. Then I noticed, at about the time I turned thirteen, my parents started getting dumber. And they continued to get dumber and dumber each and every year.

By the time I was eighteen my parents had become so stupid it was a wonder that they could survive at all. But things started looking up for my parents about the time I turned twenty-one. They slowly started getting smarter again and they have kept getting smarter and smarter as the years have gone by. Now many years later my parents are almost as smart as they were back when I was twelve years of age. You'd think that science would come up with a way for parents to retain their intelligence during their kid's teenage years but I'm not optimistic on that happening anytime soon.

Even with the cycle of parents getting smarter then dumber then smarter again, I at least had parents. So many men today grow up without a father or with a father who is absent. I not only had a father, I had a Dad. I would guess that every one of my brothers and sisters, seven of us in all, would tell you that our Dad made each of us feel special. He taught me about Faith in God, treating others respectfully, the value of hard work, the importance of generosity, to tell the truth, and to take responsibility for my actions.

Like any man, Dad was not perfect. He had a bunch of rules for us kids that were just plain silly and he was not the greatest at business…let me rephrase that…Dad was *terrible* when it came to business or financial matters. I started working in my Dad's construction business when I was in the eighth grade and I quickly learned to head to the bank as soon as my paycheck was delivered. I knew that there was a good chance that someone's check was going to bounce and I would do everything in my power make certain it wasn't mine. There were many times when I wasn't quite fast enough.

I think that Dad's business issues were due to his trusting others too much. A general contractor might owe Dad several thousand dollars on a construction contract and tell Dad that he would have the payment to him on Friday. So Dad would cut his employees their checks and hand them out on Friday morning but the check he had been promised would not arrive as expected. He believed that when someone gave their word he could literally take it to the bank.

His particular style of money management might have worked just fine if he maintained some reserves, but no such luck. If he ever did have a surplus it was spent immediately and if not by Dad then Mom would see to it. I don't pretend to know everything about my parent's financial business but for my entire life I have NEVER known my parents to have ANY savings accounts or retirement funds. NONE. EVER.

Besides his lack of business savvy Dad had other shortcomings as well. But despite his shortcomings Dad was and always will be my hero. Over the years from time to time my wife will say to me in her unflattering tone, "You are just like your Dad."

To that I will always reply, "Thank You."

When I was in tenth grade my dad was the Pastor of a small Nazarene Church in Barry, Illinois. He had been a Pastor in Sparta and Sesser, Illinois when I was younger but we moved to Colorado when I was ten years old so Dad could get a college degree. He did the college thing for a couple of years then went into the construction business when college didn't work out. Now we were back in Illinois and Dad was once again a Pastor; I was sixteen years old and still held Dad in very high regard.

At one point during this sophomore year of high school some of my siblings and I had noticed that Mom seemed to be quite upset about something. When Mom was unhappy so was everyone else. So as a matter of self-preservation we kids huddled up to try and figure out what was going on and what strategy we should employ. One of my sisters suggested that it may have something to do with a letter from an ole friend Mom had received in the previous day's mail. Something was up and we knew it. We speculated and offered our different theories on what the matter was but none of us were remotely prepared for what was about to hit us.

The next day Mom told all of us kids that later that afternoon we were having a "family meeting" and that no one would be excused for any reason. This is the first and only time I ever remembering having a "family meeting." Of course we had already been wondering what was up but now our wondering moved to a whole new level. The anticipation was killing us. Based on Mom's behavior we knew that whatever it was could not be good news.

The time *finally* arrived for the family meeting, and except for my older brother who was away serving our country in some foreign land, the entire family was present.

At the family meeting Mom wasted no time in getting to the reason for the meeting. Mom had received a letter from a friend named Dolly (not her real name). Dolly's husband worked with Dad and our families became close friends during the period when Dad worked construction. We had been to each other's homes on several occasions. This family was not what one might consider practicing "Christians" so it was quite unusual for my parents to establish such a close friendship with them.

Mom opened the letter and started reading it. She immediately started weeping. I don't remember what the letter said but in short Dad and Dolly had had an affair. After Mom stopped reading Dad, through tearful eyes, confessed that the accusation was true and he begged our forgiveness.

I will never know for certain what motivated Dolly to write that letter, or what she was hoping would result. But knowing what I know, Dad had ended the relationship shortly after it started. My guess is that Dolly felt rejected and was determined to destroy Dad as her payment in return. Indeed Dad had to resign from the church he pastored and would never pastor again.

But what I believe Dolly intended for harm actually was good for Dad. Dad knew what he had done was wrong and no doubt his secret was eating him alive. How could any man stand up in front of a congregation of people to talk about God, sin, grace and forgiveness without being tormented by his own shortcomings? The affair was out in the open and he was now free to truly experience God's mercy, grace and forgiveness.

How did learning of Dad's affair affect me? I certainly have not been without temptation nor am I immune from sexual thoughts so common to men. And even though I am no better than anyone else when it comes to sexual temptations I believe that Dad's affair has given me the resolve that I needed to keep from making the same mistake. I saw firsthand what Dad's affair did to him, his career, his marriage and his family and hopefully I have the wisdom to learn from it. Hopefully others who read this story can also learn from it.

Mom and Dad's marriage has not been without difficulty and working through the hurt caused by the affair has not been easy. But forty years later they are still together. I have never talked to Dad about the affair. Maybe I should have but for me I forgave him on the day I learned of it and have felt no need to bring it up with him again. Before now I have only even mentioned it to my wife and a couple of close friends.

Dad is a great man, I wouldn't want others to think any less of him, but our concerns about what other people think is often what keeps us from sharing our stories. But it is through sharing our stories that we are able to help others find the freedom and forgiveness that can only be found in relationship with Christ.

Courage is contagious and as we share our stories others are empowered to do the same. Because at the end of the game, we are all guilty of something; guilt and shame are the chains that keep us from freedom and forgiveness. Truth is what sets us free.

REFLECTION

1) What part of Perry's story did you identify with the most?

_____

_____

_____

_____

_____

2) In what ways has "Fatherlessness" adversely affected our culture?

_____

_____

_____

_____

_____

3) In what ways can infidelity be destructive?

_____

_____

_____

_____

_____

4) In what ways has infidelity adversely affected you or someone you know?

_____

_____

_____

_____

_____

5) Why do some men seem to be more prone to sexual temptation and infidelity than others?

_____

_____

_____

6) What advice would you offer a friend who has a hidden affair in his past?

_____

_____

_____

_____

7) At the end of this chapter Perry talks about courage being contagious and through sharing our stories we help others find freedom and forgiveness. What do you think he means by that?_____

_____

_____

_____

_____

8) What story could you tell about your life that could be helpful to others?

_____

_____

_____

_____

CHAPTER 18

The Man in the Mirror

I'M NOT A HUGE FAN of Michael Jackson. Actually, I could safely say that I'm not a fan of him at all. But as I was thinking about this chapter and came up with the title, "The Man in the Mirror" I couldn't help the nagging thought in the back of my mind that Mr. Jackson had a hit song with the same title. After a little checking my thought was confirmed and I found a stanza from that song that is worth sharing:

I'm starting with the man in the mirror
I'm asking him to change his ways
No message could have been any clearer
If you want to make the world a better place
Take a look at yourself and then make the change

I certainly can't speak for Mr. Jackson, but what little I do know about him he did not seem to be one that I would consider to be philosophical or deeply religious. But even so, the lyrics of this song seem to indicate that he understood that the world is in need of being made better and the way the world is made better is by each individual changing his ways.

In the early 1900s the London Times sent out an inquiry to famous authors, asking the question, "What's wrong with the world today?" Author and Theologian G.K. Chesterton responded simply:

> "Dear Sir: Regarding your article 'What's Wrong with the World?' I am. Yours truly,"
>
> —G.K. Chesterton

What's wrong with our world? I am.

Chesterton, like Jackson recognized that the world is in need of being made better and the only way to make the world better is by starting with oneself.

Take "hunger" or "homelessness" as examples. Many of us are content to simply ignore the problem. We pray, "Give us this day our daily bread," while the daily malnourishment of others never enters our minds. For those who cannot ignore the problem, or at least see it, we can have a number of possible responses:

- "It's not my problem."

- "It sucks to be born in a third-world country."

- "The government needs to fix this."

- "They made their bed now they can sleep in it."

- "Get a job ya lazy bum."

- "There are shelters and soup kitchens for people who need help."

As you've read in previous chapters, I grew up being poor and our family was very needy at times. Because of this I have developed a soft spot in my heart for the less fortunate. Yet on the other hand I've worked my tail off to rise above my situation. But in my self-righteousness every one of the responses listed above is a thought that I've had at one time or another when I've encountered someone in need.

I readily admit that I am probably the last person on this planet that would give money to someone standing on the street corner holding a "Will work for food" sign. I might offer them some work or a menial job; after all, that's what their asking for, right? But I have yet to have any takers on cleaning the chicken crap out of the chicken coop. I'm not too proud to clean the chicken coop and I'm not the one standing on the street corner.

My wife and I cheerfully support organizations that feed and house the less fortunate, but to me handing money to a stranger is foolishness. I only mention this to stress just how out-of-character I am in the following story.

When I lived in Grand Junction, Colorado I was in the real estate business and spent a great deal of money to make myself well-known throughout this community of 100,000 people.

My wife and I had just completed a very lavish Chinese dinner with my sister, Crystal and her husband, Bob. Bob, Crystal and my wife left the restaurant ahead of me. I was lagging behind a bit from paying the tab or using the restroom, I don't remember exactly. As they were walking across the parking lot towards our vehicles a man approached Bob. He told Bob his sob story and asked Bob for money. Bob declined the man's request but pointed towards me and told the man that he was sure that I would be more sympathetic to his condition. Bob and I have always played jokes on each other but he got me good this time. I have not yet forgiven Bob for that generous act of kindness he displayed at my expense.

This man, a complete stranger to me, walked over to me and told me this outlandish story of how he just got into town and was to start a new job - blah, blah, blah. I didn't believe this guy's story for a second. Still seething at Bob, I reached into my wallet and reluctantly gave this guy a twenty dollar bill. I wish I could tell you it was a compassionate act of kindness but I just wanted this him out of my face.

Fast forward a few more years. I received a call from a man who wanted to make an appointment for me to visit with him and his wife about selling their home. When I met with them it was clear that they wanted to sell and they seemed intent that I should be the real estate broker to do the job. It was one of the easiest listing I have ever had. I thanked them for their confidence and trust while assuring them I would do everything in my power to get their home sold.

"We wouldn't think of listing our home with anyone else," the woman stated.

"Why's that," I asked.

"A few years ago our son was living on the streets and heavy into drugs. He's clean now and has completely turned his life around, but he told us the story of how he 'panhandled' you one time in the parking lot of a Chinese restaurant. We don't know what would have happened if you hadn't given him that money, but we like to think that you and all the other people he took money from played a role in saving his life; for that we are extremely grateful." She went on and filled me in on a few of the details of her son's story and how far he had come.

As she was telling me this story I remembered the incident vividly. I remembered it not because I was compassionate and generous, but because of the awkward situation my brother-in-law had put me in. As she told me this story I was quite humbled. It made me realize that in every situation there is so much more than we will ever know and that in some small way we are all connected. I retold them the story from my perspective and confessed that I was not the hero they were making me out to be. But for them my motivation was not at issue. To them I had helped save their son and nothing would convince them otherwise.

I still think handing money to strangers is foolish and I now have an even greater appreciation for homeless shelters and soup kitchens. I think it is easy to look at the problems of our world and become paralyzed when we see the enormity of the problems. But I love the wisdom of Mother Teresa when she said, "If you can't feed a hundred people, then feed just one."

As we grow older, hopefully we will also grow wiser. And if we hope to leave this world a better place we will see our own personal need to change. So if indeed we must change for the world to become a better place, how do we go about that? What does change really look like?

First, I believe that the potential to change the world is within the heart of every man.

Second, I believe that the attempts to change us by our wives, friends, family, employers or even God Himself are of no avail until we longingly desire to be changed. Unfortunately our desire to be changed is most often preceded by intense pain. It seems we need a cancer diagnosis or a heart attack before we're willing to change unhealthy habits.

Third, a man's most innate need is to have purpose and make a difference. Yet when it comes to the kind of change within us that is needed to make the world a better place, it will never happen within our own power. Our desire to change is crucial, but our desire alone is not enough. We, as world-changing men, are totally useless until we embrace the purpose that God has for our lives. If our purpose is indeed "God-given," I assure you that our purpose will be in the service of others rather than in pursuit of things to gratify ourselves.

Regardless of how "successful" they might have been in their pursuit, history rarely remembers fondly those whose pursuits were fame, power, wealth or sex. The greatest men who are fondly remembered throughout history are those who gave of their time, intellect and wealth to make the lives of others less painful.

I'm the first to admit that I am a work in progress. Just about the time I get one defect corrected or complete, I recognize yet another attitude adjustment or glaring deficiency. I am fully convinced that this process for me will be unending as long as I remain a resident of this planet. However, when I was in my mid-thirties I saw the need to begin this life-changing process. Sure, I had been a Christian my entire life but I looked at the man in the mirror and what I saw I did not like. With God's help I wanted to change.

I made a list of "Ten Rules to Live By" that I'll share with you. The funny thing about rules is that they are usually *someone else's* idea as to how we should live our lives. But if our rules are our own rules and in collaboration with God's rules and His purpose for our lives then we have ownership in them and are much more inclined to comply. I think it ultimately gets down to really believing what we say we believe.

These rules are *for me*; they are not intended to tell you how you should live. If any of these rules resonate with you then feel free to use them, but I have no right or desire to push my rules onto anyone else. I have carried this list in my Bible for years and will give them to you in reverse order of how I have them listed.

Rule number ten: Goals without plans are useless. This rule is a product of my experience in the business world. Many of us write personal or business goals or at least think about New Year's Resolutions. My experience has been that very few people take the time to write down their goals. So to find someone who has written goals AND a plan to reach those goals is indeed rare. This rule applies to my spiritual life just as much as it has to my business and personal life because they cannot be separated from each other. My most innate need, the need for my life to have purpose and truly make a difference is only met through seeking and finding what God's purpose is for my life. But I have found that if I indeed know God's purpose or *goals* for my life He will also provide the necessary *plan* to fulfill His purposes and goals.

Rule number nine: There is no such thing as a 50/50 partnership. When I have shared this rule from time to time I often get pushback from people claiming that their business or their marriage is the exception. There are no exceptions. Another misconception about this rule is that it is a bad thing to be on the short side of the partnership; not only is it not a bad thing but is actually necessary. Nothing would ever get decided or accomplished if 50/50 partnerships existed. Whether in business, marriage or even friendship, for it to work, someone has to be in charge and someone must be willing to accept a supporting role. Both are equally important. This also applies to my relationship with God and for this relationship to work I must regularly remind myself…He > I.

Rule number eight: Don't offer an opinion unless it is asked for but when I'm asked my opinion I'm to give an honest one. The two exceptions to this rule have been my children before they became adults and my employees when my silence could be costly.

Abraham Lincoln once said, "Better to remain silent and be thought a fool than to speak and remove all doubt." This piece of wisdom fits me to a tee. When I participate in group meetings and discussions, sometimes I manage to produce an absolutely brilliant comment while other times I have demonstrated my ability to say things that are utterly ridiculous. My problem is that before I open my mouth I have no idea which option is about to come out. For me the safest plan is to just remain silent unless my opinion is required.

Another aspect of this rule is that I, like everyone else, have feelings, opinions, ideas and thoughts. But there is a time to share them and a time to keep them to myself. Wisdom is knowing the difference.

Every group has someone who dominates the discussion and talks so much that we get to the point where we tune them out every time they begin to speak. If you are part of a group and no one comes to mind as being one who dominates the conversation, well…I hate to say this…buuut…think about it.

Rule number seven: Don't complain; if I have a problem fix it. If I can't fix it then I will live with it the best I can. I've had problems like everyone else and I want to fix things like anyone else. Fixing problems and eliminating discomfort is healthy and good. But I have learned not to be discouraged by adversity. Every cloud has a silver lining and every problem is an opportunity. This is really hard to embrace while I'm in the middle of difficulty, but it is indeed true. But if I can't seem to find that silver lining I must remind myself that I can't stand being around complainers and I sure don't want to be perceived as being one myself.

Rule number six: Be thankful: if I must compare myself to others compare myself to those less fortunate. I have been to Monte Carlo, Monaco and I cannot imagine a place where such abundant wealth could be more obvious. I truly felt like a fish out of water and it would be so easy to become dissatisfied and discouraged when I compare my meager existence to those who hang out there. But I have also been to places that are extremely impoverished where it is just as easy to be content and humbly grateful for my same meager existence. I'll take contentment and humble gratitude over dissatisfaction and discontent any day of the week.

Rule number five: Treat every conversation as if it was being recorded; don't talk about others negatively. I'm not perfect and I break my own rules occasionally. No breaking of my rules gets me in more trouble than when I blow this one. I believe that we all come with a filter positioned within our head somewhere between our brain and our mouth. I control the switch that turns my filter on or off. We all know people that go through their entire life with their filter turned off. Nothing good has ever happened to me when I've had my filter in the off position. Enough said.

Rule number four: Don't be a fool; if something sounds too good to be true assume that it is. This rule is about knowing that there are men out there who are after things and that they will try to draw me into their schemes in whatever way that suites them. This rule is a reminder to use wisdom. But the danger in this rule is that it has probably made me a bit more cynical than what I should be. If one extreme is cynicism, then the other is naiveté. I prefer to lean towards cynicism. By doing so it means passing on a few good deals to avoid all of the bad ones. To quote a well-known business expression; "Ain't no such thing as a free lunch."

Rule number three: When it comes to finances, contribute the tithe (10%), save the tithe (10%) and learn to live on the remainder (80%). Don't borrow money to buy something that I can live without. For me this rule is about living within my means, saving a little so that I won't be a burden to others and being faithful in generosity. I could write an entire book on this rule and as a matter of fact a lot of people have done just that.

When I was younger I was into acquiring stuff just as much as anyone else. I believed a lie and convinced myself, "You work hard, you deserve it." The truth is that I was never satisfied no matter how much stuff I had. The same is true for people who worship wealth; no matter how much they have they will never have enough. I have come to realize that every material possession I own will someday find its way to a landfill. True satisfaction comes through serving and helping others.

Rule number two: Do unto others as you would have them do unto you. I considered writing this rule to say, "Love your neighbor as yourself." No matter how I phrase it, for me, this rule is the toughest rule of them all. For me treating others as I want to be treated is at least doable. But loving my neighbor as myself, for me, is impossible. I can usually treat others the way I'd like to be treated. But with the *possible* exceptions of my wife and children, I can't think of any "neighbors" or any person for that matter that I love as myself. God's rule to "Love my neighbor as myself" is beyond my comprehension. As a matter of fact, if these rules were just *my* rules it probably wouldn't even have made my list. No matter how impossible this rule may seem I must seek God's help and continue to make every effort to live by it. This rule must remain on my list because rule number one demands it.

Rule number one: Love the Lord your God with all of your heart, soul, mind and strength. Some may claim that this rule is not my rule but rather is another one of *God's rules*. They may claim that it is *His idea* of how I should live my life rather than *my idea* of how I should live my life. This claim is indeed partly true, but it is not entirely true. **Love the Lord your God with all of your**

heart, soul, mind and strength is God's number one rule, it is His rule or command that encapsulates all of His other rules and commands. However, God is gracious and will not force Himself on me or anyone else; I must be a willing participant. *I had* to surrender to Him. *I had* to accept his love, forgiveness and mercy. He stood knocking at my door, but *I had* to open it. *I had* to make His number one rule my number one rule…will you?

REFLECTION

1) What part of Perry's story did you identify with the most?

    _____

    _____

    _____

    _____

    _____

2) When you look at the man in the mirror what do you see that needs to change?

    _____

    _____

    _____

    _____

    _____

3) What purpose has God given you for your life?

    _____

    _____

    _____

    _____

    _____

4) In what ways could you do more to serve the needs of others?

    _____

    _____

    _____

    _____

    _____

5) Make a list of your own rules for you to live by

_____

_____

_____

_____

_____

6) What does it mean to "Love your neighbor as yourself"?

_____

_____

_____

_____

_____

7) If you were to truly love the Lord your God with all your heart, soul, mind and strength, in what ways would your life change?

_____

_____

_____

_____

_____

CHAPTER 19

The Elephant in the Room

THOUGHT I WAS DONE WRITING this book. I met with my friend and editor, Rob Fischer, and proudly proclaimed, "It is finished." Knowing my sense of accomplishment that accompanied the thrill of completing an enormous task, he graciously convinced me that the book needed one more chapter. Like having a penalty on the final play of a very close football game, my elation was postponed.

Rob said that there was one particular men's issue that had been subtly addressed throughout this book but he felt that the issue needed to be dealt with more directly. He said, "It's like an elephant in the room that affects millions of men yet no one wants to talk about it." He advised me not to dance around the issue but to deal with it head-on.

So before I deal with this issue, please allow me the indulgence of one more story.

Throughout this book I've touched on the various phases of my working history but here I'd like to offer a recap so you have the proper context of where I'm headed. When I was in eighth grade I began working in the family construction business and continued to do so on weekends, holidays and summer vacations until I graduated from college. After college my wife and I took a job managing seventy-two apartment units and did this for just over one year. After managing the apartments, I accepted a position as Office Manager for a group of physicians. I held this position for about three years.

Next, I started a financial consulting business which evolved into a real estate business. This was my profession for almost thirty years. About five years before getting out of the real estate business I launch an internet marketing business. I eventually sold the real estate business so that I could devote full time to the internet marketing business which has since shut down. I still believe that the internet marketing concept we launched is far and away better than any internet marketing business operating today. But the million dollars invested in the business by me and a few friends was far too little to carry the company to the tipping point. Other than the money we lost and the hit to my pride, there was no serious damage as a result.

After shutting down the internet marketing business I began doing business consulting work. Basically companies would hire me to look at whatever seemed to be troubling them and I would develop strategies to cure their ailment. Most problems can be reduced to one of three things: a policy, a practice, or a person. Sometimes solving my client's problem would involve knocking off a competitor or breaking the legs of their employees' union representative. Just kidding.

One of my business consulting clients was a Pregnancy Resource Center. The leadership of this organization seemed convinced that most, if not all women and men involved in an abortion were adversely affected by it. Yet in their city where abortions numbered

2000 annually, only fifteen to twenty women each year attended any sort of post-abortion recovery/healing group. Typically, the number of men participating in these groups each year was zero.

After reviewing their problem I came to the conclusion that there were three *possible reasons* why so few people were participating in post-abortion healing programs. Either:

1) My client was incorrect in their assumption that most people involved in abortions are adversely affected, or…

2) Post-abortive individuals were unaware of their need for my client's services, or…

3) Post-abortive individuals saw their need for my client's services but were unaware that my client offered these services.

If item #1 were true it would simply be a matter doing some research and providing some answers. If items #2 or #3 were true it would be a matter of developing a more effective marketing strategy.

I surmised that another possible reason for low participation could be ineffective curriculum but ruled that possibility out due to lack of participants to begin with. However, it was clear that none of the few post-abortive group participants were returning to subsequent groups, bringing with them a post-abortive friend or family member. This was an indication that the curriculum may indeed be an issue. In other words, as with any business, there is usually some sort of problem if existing clients are not referring other clients to that business.

For eight months I read everything I could get my hands on related to the topic of abortion. I conducted several focus groups of post-abortive women. I heard or read dozens if not hundreds of stories of men and women involved in an abortion. And I came to the following conclusions:

1) **No person, man or woman, has been involved in an abortion experience without being adversely affected.** Of the hundreds of abortion stories I have heard I have yet to hear a single one where the abortion participant *did not* develop some sort of behavioral issue *after* the experience. My client's assumption was correct.

2) I do not claim or pretend to be any sort of behavioral expert, but I have done enough research and have interviewed enough people to know that what I'm about to say is undoubtedly true. Some of the more common post-abortive behavioral issues I've seen include: abuse of alcohol; addictions to sex, pornography, legal and illegal drugs or gambling; sleep disorders; excessive or unhealthy drive to excel at work, school or sports, excessive pro-life or pro-choice activism; anger issues; a change from a heterosexual to a gay or lesbian lifestyle; and an aversion to being around children or pregnant women. But the interesting thing about the people I have spoken with is that *they rarely recognize the connection between their abortion and their behavioral deviations.* And many do not see their behavioral deviations as a problem at all; they simply chalk it up as who they are. **In short, people do not readily see their need for post-abortion healing because they see their behavioral issue as the problem rather than their behavioral issue being a symptom of the underlying abortion.** My client had a marketing problem.

3) It is very rare when someone who abuses alcohol wakes up one morning and says to himself, "Self, you have an alcohol addiction. You need to enroll in Alcoholics Anonymous." Before attending any program to get away from the alcohol he must first reach a breaking point. He must first encounter the potential loss of something he

values more than the alcohol. Among other things, this could be his marriage, his job, his ability to drive, or his reputation. The same is true of any other addiction or behavioral issue. To effectuate change of behavior people must be "pushed" or "compelled" to make the change. Abortion recovery is no different. Organizations can advertise, promote and market post-abortion recovery programs until they are blue in the face but the results will remain dismal. **It does no good to invite people to a post-abortive recovery group; people must be brought to a group by someone who loves them enough to make it happen.** This too is an issue that must be resolved through a more effective marketing strategy.

Another discovery I made in my abortion research is that the people who indeed were able to move past their abortion experience all had three things in common. First, they attended any one of a number of post-abortion recovery programs. Second, there was always an element of forgiveness from God and the ability to forgive themselves. Third, there was some sort of deliberate acknowledgement of the humanity of the aborted child and an intentional grieving process.

All this I learned while doing research for my client, the Pregnancy Resource Center. But now I was in a quandary. I learned that poor participation in post-abortion recovery groups was not only the experience of my client but that poor attendance in post-abortion recovery groups was almost universal. This problem was common in every major US city as well as cities all over the world.

Then I heard that very quiet yet forceful voice in my head saying, "Now that you know what you know, what are you going to do about it?"

The argument was on. I felt that God wanted me to create an organization for the post-abortive modeled after the granddaddy of all anonymous organizations, Alcoholics Anonymous. I *did not* want to do this. God and I argued. I lost the argument. So in 2013 I founded an organization, Abortion Anonymous, Inc. (AbAnon). More about AbAnon can be found at http://www.abanon.org.

When starting AbAnon, my original intention was to simply serve on the Board of Directors for a period of time to help get it started then I would get out of the way. I thought then, and still do today that the Executive Director of AbAnon needs to be an articulate, attractive, educated, post-abortive, woman. I strike out on all five characteristics. But God and our Board of Directors, in their infinite wisdom, have placed me in this position for a season.

Now, back to my friend Rob Fischer and the elephant in the room.

I'm sure you have figured out by now but the elephant in the room that no one seems to want to talk about is the devastation caused by abortion and the role we men have played in allowing it to happen.

When it comes to abortion, I believe that many men have acted selfishly or cowardly. Selfishly, because we've put our dreams, pride and desires above our God-given responsibility to provide and protect. Cowardly, because we won't speak the truth about abortion because we fear what others will think or say about us.

Some of you reading this book are of the opinion that abortion is a good thing and are clueless as to how wrong and evil it is. You might consider yourself to be pro-choice and proud of it. I even know of pro-choice ministers and priests. If this describes you, then I would challenge you to open your heart and mind by reading a few books that offer an opinion contrary to yours. One such book is a book which I've written titled *Change the Shame; Continuing the Battle for Civil Rights.*

Some of you reading this book are probably of the opinion that most abortions are wrong but you are okay with abortion if the mother was raped or the child has a disability. If you fit this category, I offer the same challenge I gave the men described in the paragraph above. As humans we tend to believe whatever we choose to believe regardless of how overwhelming the evidence is to the contrary. But if our hearts and minds are open God can change them.

Undoubtedly, some of you reading this book are pro-life but, like I used to be, you are closet pro-lifers. I was pro-life but I wasn't about to say anything to anyone that might create an awkward situation or put me in a bad light. Quite honestly, I was a coward about what other people thought; especially when it came to people I did business with.

Some of you reading this book are pro-life and vocal about being so. But I can only applaud your pro-life position if it is accompanied by compassion, love and forgiveness towards those who have been involved in an abortion. We have all done things we are not proud of. Something about casting stones comes to mind. Spouting God's *grace* without understanding one's *guilt* is just as worthless as critically pointing out *one's guilt* without offering His *grace.* Both scenarios are equally ineffective.

Some of you reading this book may have fathered a child and your child was aborted without you knowing about it until it was too late. I can only imagine the pain, anger or helplessness you must have felt. My hope is that you can process those emotions properly and come to the point where you are able to forgive your child's mother.

Some of you reading this book were quiet bystanders while your wife, girlfriend or daughter had an abortion and you said nothing or did very little to defend the child. You bought into the lie that abortion is a woman's health issue and since you don't have a uterus you must keep your mouth shut and your opinions to yourself. But just as women have maternal instincts to nurture and care, men have paternal instincts to provide and protect. I've learned from so many testimonials that to stand by and do nothing while your child or grandchild is taken can haunt you for your entire life.

Some of you reading this book were active participants in an abortion. You may have begged, coerced, manipulated or even forced your wife, girlfriend or daughter into having an abortion. You may have paid for the abortion, driven the car to the clinic or were present during the procedure. Perhaps the details surrounding the event that happened many years ago are burned into your memory as if they had taken place yesterday. You may still be trying to convince yourself that it was the right thing to do and justify your actions. But deep within your soul you know that what you did was wrong.

Man or woman, those who have played a role in an abortion will never be all that God intends them to be until they have properly processed the abortion and found forgiveness, healing and freedom. The enemy wants you to quietly remain in your shame and guilt. You see, the enemy knows that once you are set free, your story has the power to free dozens or possibly hundreds of other men.

If you have been a bystander or have actively played a role in an abortion, I want to encourage you participate in a post-abortion recovery program for men. I know, you're probably thinking, "I'm tough and I've dealt with it in my own way." You may know that you have been forgiven by God, and you may have even forgiven yourself. But my guess is that unless you've been part of a post-abortion recovery group, you have not properly dealt with your abortion. If this is the case, there are probably some behavioral issues that you struggle with on a regular basis. If that's true of you, attend a group to help yourself. If I am mistaken, great, attend such a group to help others.

Contact your church or a local Pregnancy Resource Center and ask if they have an **AbAnon Group** for men. If not, encourage them to start one, or better yet, consider starting one yourself. Information about AbAnon can be found at AbAnon.org.

REFLECTION

1) What part of Perry's story did you identify with the most?

_____

_____

_____

_____

_____

2) List three things you learned about abortion from this chapter.

_____

_____

_____

_____

3) This chapter contained several descriptions of, "Some of you reading this book." Which of these descriptions most closely describes you?_____

_____

_____

_____

_____

4) If you have been involved with an abortion, now that you know what you know, what are you going to do about it? Who will hold you accountable?

_____

_____

_____

_____

_____

5) Of the men that you know well, who do you know has been involved in an abortion? What will you do to help these men find forgiveness and healing?

_____

_____

_____

_____

_____

6) If you have been involved in an abortion, how could sharing your story benefit others?

_____

_____

_____

_____

_____

7) Refer back to the Introduction at the beginning of this book. If a movie was to be made about your life, what changes do you need to make that will make your life a story that others will find worth watching?

_____

_____

_____

_____

_____

Made in the USA
Columbia, SC
01 November 2018